SECRETS OF AN UPWORK MASTER

A Freelancer's Guide to Thriving on the Upwork Platform

Josh Burnett

Triple-V Publishing

Corvallis, Oregon

Upwork is a trademark of Upwork Global Inc and is being used without permission. No challenge to any trademark's status is express or implied. Neither this book nor any associated training materials have been produced, designed, or approved by Upwork.

Copyright © 2020 Josh Burnett

All rights reserved.

Book Interior and E-book Design by Amit Dey

Disclaimers

Terms & Conditions: Please review Upwork's terms & conditions before applying any of the strategies outlined in this book. This book reflects a snapshot in time, while terms and conditions can change quickly. I have made every effort to accurately represent the products and services I have used. However, these are subject to my interpretation.

Earnings: This book is provided for informational and educational purposes only. I make no warranty or guarantee, implied or express, that you will see the same results I have experienced and described here. The results you have are subject to numerous independent factors that vary from reader to reader, including many that are outside of your control. Any examples I provide should not be interpreted as a guarantee of earnings. I cannot and do not offer financial or legal advice and nothing in this book should be taken or construed as such. While the publisher and author have exerted their best efforts in the preparation of this book, neither make any representations or warranties with respect to the accuracy or completeness of the contents of this book and specifically disclaim any implied warranties or merchantability or fitness for a particular purpose and any liability for any misuse or damages stemming from the contents of this book.

*To the four reasons who have kept me going
through thick and thin.
You're why I wake up every morning.
I love you.*

Table of Contents

Introduction ix
What Clients Say About Josh xi

Chapter One: Finding Your Niche 1
    The Freedom of Freelancing 1
    What You'll Learn 2
    The Traffic of Craigslist, the Professionalism of LinkedIn . . . 4
    Start with Tasks 5
    How a Client Lists a Job 6
    Freelancer Categories 7
    Other Freelancing Platforms 12
    Upwork Freelancing Plans 13
    Chapter One Exercise 20

Chapter Two: Anatomy of an Ad 21
    Optimizing Your Job Feed 21
    Using Filtered Search 22
    What a Freelancer Sees 28
    What a Client Sees 38
    Chapter Two Exercise 44

Chapter Three: Optimizing Your Profile 47
    Making a Good First Impression 48
    How to Structure Your Profile 50
    The Five Don'ts of Overviews 57
    How the JSS is Calculated 73
    How Contracts are Weighted 74
    Avoiding JSS Pitfalls 75
    If You Encounter Problems 78
    Recovering from a Poor JSS 81
    The Crucial Role of Timing 84
    How to Explain a Poor JSS 85
    The Benefits of a Good JSS 86
    Keeping Your JSS Stable 87
    Chapter Three Exercise 88

Chapter Four: Finding the Right Contract 89
    How to Use Search Filters to Find the Perfect Job. 90
    Critiquing an Ad 93
    What to Look for in a Client 100
    Evaluating a Job Posting 101
    Evaluating the "About the client" Section. 106
    Understanding Service Fees 112
    Chapter Four Exercise 113

Chapter Five: Placing a Winning Bid 115
    The Material for Your Cover Letter 115
    Drafting a Master Cover Letter 116
    The Final Paragraph 119

Table of Contents

Nailing the Intro Paragraph. 120
Plug and Play from the JAT 121
Using Work Samples 122
Responding to Invitations 124
Handling Screening Questions 125
Default Responses 126
Handling Interview Invitations 131
Keeping Everything on Upwork 132
Pre-Interview Prep 133
Conducting the Interview 135
Declined Bids. 136
Bidding Strategies 137
Managing Non-Traditional Job Offers 139
Summary 140
Chapter Five Exercise 141

Chapter Six: Executing a Contract Successfully 143

Clarifying Expectations 143
Putting the Client's Satisfaction First 145
Taking the Blame 146
Honesty is Always the Best Policy 146
Developing the Right Mindset 148
When Things Go Well 149
How to be Successful with Fixed-Price Work 151
Approaching Hourly Work Correctly 152
When Things Go Badly 154
Working Through a Dispute 156

    Where Negative Feedback Appears 160

    Preventing Negative Feedback 162

    Removing Negative Feedback 165

    Responding to Negative Feedback 166

    How to Leave Negative Feedback 169

    What Appropriate Negative Feedback Looks Like 170

    How to Write Negative Feedback 171

    Using Negative Feedback to Identify Bad Clients 172

    Chapter Six Exercise. 174

Chapter Seven: Thriving. 179

    Getting Paid 180

    Maintaining a Consistent, Stable Workflow 181

    Enjoying Contract Perks 184

    Earning the Top-Rated Badge 186

    Developing Symbiotic Relationships with Other Freelancers . 187

    Using the Upwork Community 189

    Working with Agencies 190

    Chapter Seven Exercise 191

Epilogue 195

The Importance of Tenacity 195

About the Author 201

Introduction

I'm publishing this book as COVID-19 is sweeping the globe. Social distancing has wreaked havoc on the economy and perhaps your life, personally. Freelancing is never something I considered until I was forced into it. It was a scary moment. I stepped into a complete unknown, using a skill I had no formal training in, exploring an occupation that had never previously crossed my mind.

Freelancing isn't a "get rich quick" scheme. Independent contracting doesn't involve any kind of network marketing. For most people, there won't be any expansion; you won't preside over a vast empire of people working for you. Instead, what I'll promise you is hard work--if you're a typical employee from corporate America, as I was, this is nothing like you've ever done before. There is going to be frustration and discouragement. You'll feel like a failure often. You'll need humility and patience to admit when something you're trying isn't working and have to revamp your whole approach.

But what's on the other side is priceless: freedom.

When the rest of the economy shut down, I logged into my computer and began work like every other weekday morning. I sipped my coffee as I perused the job listings, bid on a few that interested me, then got to work on a research paper for a client.

In the months before schools closed, I recognized that my kids needed a bit of extra attention from me--they'd been through a lot of transition and were looking for extra stability. I changed my work hours and began eating lunch with them every day at school. I can take days off when I need them; start work early if I wake up before my alarm or finish my efforts late if that's how the day needs to go. If I have a project or a purchase I'm saving for, I can ramp up my work schedule for a few weeks and pay it off.

Most importantly, though, I have the confidence to know that I'm going to be able to provide for my family, come what may--and that's a peace I never had before. Amid all the tumult and disruptions caused by this nasty little virus, I hope that you can find something in my story that will help you to take a step toward achieving that independence.

—Josh Burnett

www.UpworkMasters.com

What Clients Say About Josh

KNOCKED. IT. OUT. OF. THE. PARK.

Outstanding content writer, enthusiast and engaged partner. Highly recommend

Great guy, went over the top at each stage, worked well with my way of thinking and yet gave good guidance. No battling egos which often occur with a team situation of this sort. Will hire again to be sure!! Thanks Josh!!!

Josh is an extremely strong technical writer, even with topics he hasn't written about before. His quality of writing, research prowess and ability to adapt is nothing short of exceptional.

Josh provided extremely helpful and detailed information. Very impressive!

Josh is my lead News editor and team manager and does a phenomenal job managing, writing & editing - top-notch skills and work ethic.

Let's just say this, I hired Joshua for one job, and I have already hired him for 3 others already. He is the best copywriter here on Upwork. I consider him one of my team now. Do not hesitate to work with Joshua, you won't be disappointed.

Josh is great at communication and ensuring tasks are clearly understood and that he is delivering per expectations and requirements. He's also willing to go the extra mile to ensure a top-notch deliverable!

Simply excellent.

Josh does great work. He was consummate professional while being incredibly flexible with our team.

So glad that I found Josh. He is easy to work with, easy to communicate with and produces top-quality work very quickly. One last attribute - he has successfully tackled projects from a wide array of topic areas with equal aplomb.

Joshua has provided me the best experience on Upwork thus far. His ability to take very little information and then flawlessly execute content that speaks to the right audience is amazing. He incorporated all the right pieces in all the right places and we couldn't be happier with the result. Not to mention, the turnaround time was super-fast. I'll definitely be trying to pick him up for future jobs.

Joshua promptly communicated with me and delivered anything I requested with the most sensitive, thorough and creative aspects of a job.

I never imagined LinkedIn summary could be so inspiring....

Will love to work with him again and definitely recommend to others.

Josh is amazing, will work with him again any time!

Joshua is an excellent copy writer that is able to write on minimal instructions and from my lack of communication. He's been our go to guy from product descriptions, to articles.

I wouldn't hesitate to hire him again. Best wishes and we wish you nothing but the best on your new endeavors!

Josh is an absolute pleasure to work with. Communication between us is very easy and he always incorporates my changes and suggestions into future work efforts. I never have to share the same suggestions twice. My only hesitation in recommending him so highly is that his availability will shrink!

Amazing work! We are hiring Josh for another position and look forward to continued success!

Josh has just been amazing. I have never worked with someone as competent as him. I extremely enjoyed with him. Words cannot describe how satisfied I am and how great it was to work with him!!

 # He respected every deadline (he actually overperformed and returned everything well in advance).

 # The quality was just outstanding... He is truly a professional!!

 # He was always available, able to work at short notice and provide an almost instant output with extreme quality

 # When I was busy and couldn't give him input, he used his self problem-solving skills and advanced the project... and the results were just incredible!

He is amazing to work with!!

He became my go-to person for any type of writing/research now. I would recommend him for any type of writing/research. I have no doubt he will over-deliver!!

THANK YOU JOSH!!!

Adding Josh to my team has allowed me to scale my publishing business more than I ever had previously. I know I can always count on him to produce work that makes both me and my authors look great.

Joshua is a fabulous writer. He delivered on time and exceeded our expectations.

Great work, responsive to deadlines and feedback, will work with again asap!

Everything about Josh was fantastic! I've never seen someone as ethical (he will do what's right for you and will conduct himself according to the highest values), motivated and committed to someone else's success as Josh.

I can recommend personally that he is the best you can find on this platform for any kind of work you can imagine! He is the best! Thanks Josh for everything!
You made this for me!

Joshua is very well versed in his profession. Great communication and information provided as requested. I highly recommend.

Josh did a great job. He listens to feedback, asks good questions, and genuinely cares about the final product -- he's not just spitting out a draft and collecting the money.

Josh was fantastic! He is very professional and really came through, adhering to the project parameters and deadline. He is definitely worth what he charges, and then some. I highly recommend Josh to any one looking for a stellar copywriter!

Josh is a "rare find" in the freelance writing world. His writing skills are incredible and he understands people. This is an area most writers get wrong and will certainly be working with him again. Speed, attention to detail, and creativity are traits that you'll find working with Josh.

Extraordinarily talented, an unbeatable work ethic, consistently rapid responses, honest feedback, and a genuine pleasure to work with. It is an understatement to say that Josh possesses each of these qualities. If you've sent him an offer to work together, you've certainly made the right choice. I'm extremely grateful for his expertise!

Joshua is very professional. When we talked over the phone, he explained the project details very clearly. He kept his word and delivered excellence. When his clients say "Can I give you six stars", I actually believe it because he truly deserves six stars. Great Job Joshua.

Josh is the best you can find on this platform. Thanks to him I got into HARVARD! I am so glad and happy that I have worked with him on this platform. He changed my life! Words can't describe how satisfied I am with his work. He is the kind of person that you wish you could rate him 10 stars! And even that wouldn't do justice to him!

He is extremely smart, dedicated, ethical and committed to your success! I have never seen someone as committed to your project as him. He is straight as an arrow. He will do more than overdelivering. Following my experience with Josh, I can confidently say that if he says he can do your work - he will blow your mind.

I can't thank him enough or express my gratitude for him in this box!!! THANK YOU!

Josh was our rockstar chief editor and News manager for 2 of our companies. He fully managed the news team (hiring, training, managing, editing) and ran the news department like it was his own company. Unfortunately, we had to retire the news dept due to some Google updates in the health industry. It felt like he was in the office with us, even though he was halfway across the country.
We can't recommend Josh enough for anyone looking for a top-notch hire.

It was a pleasure working with Josh. Great talent - always exceeded expectations! His outcome was outstanding while the input I gave him was always limited. I strongly recommend him!

Josh is incredible. We hired him to help with assessment writing project management and he went above in beyond. He's helped us recruiting and hiring, coordinating complex projects, market research, and much more. He is always pleasant to work with and delivers phenomenal work.

I cannot recommend him enough.

CHAPTER ONE

Finding Your Niche

I think everyone should have an Upwork account. Even if you're completely satisfied with your job and never plan on leaving it, every person I know would occasionally like the ability to pull in some extra cash, on demand, and have complete control over when that happens. ***Freelancing is not exclusively for those who choose to do it full time.*** In fact, McKinsey Global performed a study on "the gig economy" in 2016 and found that between 20 and 30 percent of the working-age population in the United States and Western Europe, or more than 160 million individuals, perform freelance work in some capacity.

The Freedom of Freelancing

It's easy to see why. McKinsey defined those who do independent work by three outstanding features: "(1) a high degree of autonomy; (2) payment by task, assignment, or sales; and (3) a short-term relationship between worker and client." One thing all freelancers share is the desire to be our own bosses, even if it's just for a few hours a month. We want to be able to set our own course, steer our own ship, and have more freedom, whether by the nature of the job or the fact that you can choose to increase your income whenever you damn well please.

We also want to feel like we're making a difference: there's a lot to be said for the feeling of accomplishment you get when you complete a task or a project. Working with clients typically involves a defined objective with a clear starting point and a specific end result, allowing you to feel like you're getting something done every single day. There's an immediate connection between your effort and the income it produces. You'll experience a childlike nostalgia that brings you back to your lawn-mowing, leaf-raking, babysitting-for-extra-cash days. Trading excess time for money has never felt sweeter.

Finally, who hasn't wished they could fire their boss at one point or another? The fantastic thing about freelancing is that you get to try out multiple bosses on short-term projects, and the ones you like, you can cultivate relationships with for follow-up contracts. Imagine being able to cull clients to the point where you're only working with the top three bosses you've ever had--what would that be worth to you?

None of this is a pipe dream. This can absolutely happen to you. I've experienced it in my own life, and I know multiple freelancers in the same position. It isn't easy, though--you're gonna have to work for every bit of it. I can't do this for you: if you've got a skill or a product and you're willing to put in the effort, I can show you how to be successful.

What You'll Learn

If you're interested, let me show you how it's done. At this point, I assume that you've already created an Upwork account and have explored the platform to some degree. If you haven't, check out my previous book, *Freelancing Foundations*. Because success on

Upwork rests on understanding how the platform works and what clients are looking for, this course is set up in four major stages:

1. **I'll walk you through how a client posts a job.** This is where the whole process starts: with someone who has work to be done. The section will introduce what they're looking for, various factors that tie into how a client finds freelancers, and how to position yourself to meet their precise needs.

2. After you've developed an appreciation of how contracts are created and posted, **I'll guide you through a complete scrub of your Upwork profile.** You'll learn common do's and don'ts, how each piece of your profile correlates to finding work, and how to optimize each section to maximize your chances of success.

3. Now that you understand both pieces of the puzzle (the client and the contractor sides), it's time to put them together. **This is where we'll cover the bidding process**: I'll work through finding the right job, deciding whether to bid, writing and submitting your cover letter, dealing with supplemental questions, handling interviews and negotiations, and executing the contract.

4. At this point, it's time to thrive. Your profile is created, and you're actively bidding, you understand how to land contracts, and now **it's time to really make Upwork work for you.** We'll walk through goal setting (is this short-term, supplemental income for you, or do you want to make it a career?), pricing strategies (when do you give yourself a raise, how much should you increase, and what are the catalysts and warning signs for this?), and customer service (knowing all of the Upwork mechanisms for client interactions is crucial to long-term success).

The Traffic of Craigslist, the Professionalism of LinkedIn

This is my favorite way to describe Upwork. You'll be surprised (and perhaps a little shocked) at some of the jobs you find. I was once hired to catalog all of the escort services in a major city, breaking down their business models, recruitment methods, and payment mechanisms. I haven't seen so many boobies in such a short period since... well, it's been a while. I've been hired to research the impact of climate change-induced sea-level rise on twelve specific cities around the globe. There are job posts that want you to review a smartphone app, others that want you to be a product tester, and some where clients simply want to pick your brain about hobbies you have as they conduct market research. And it's call carried out in an impressively professional environment.

What can I do?? This is the most common first question I get when I talk to someone about freelancing. We all tend to have a dimmer view of our skillset than is accurate, and I promise you, there's something for everyone on this platform. Do you believe that you're just a glorified office shill? Think again. If you've ever designed a PowerPoint presentation, put formulas into a spreadsheet, or reorganized a shared drive, there's work for you. Can you pick up a phone, dial a business, and ask a question? There are jobs you're qualified for.

It's normal to doubt whether you have any marketable skills--but it's equally inaccurate. I've done quite a bit of hiring in some of my project manager roles, and here's a brief list of positions I've hired:

- Bartender
- CNC Machinist
- Hotel Cleaner
- HVAC Installer
- Accountant
- Call Center Technicians
- Construction Workers
- Caregivers

- Line Cooks
- Adult Caregivers
- Data Entry Clerk
- Dental Assistant
- Medical Assistant
- Veterinary Assistant
- Hotel Front Desk Agent
- Server
- Forklift Operator
- Graphic Designers
- Writers
- Hairstylist
- Phlebotomist
- Medical Biller
- Mechanic
- Hydraulic Technician
- Social Media Manager
- Middle School Teacher
- Elementary School Teacher
- High School Teacher
- Registered Nurse
- Office Manager
- Software Developer
- Cashier
- Personal Trainer
- Computer Programmer
- Receptionist
- Retail Merchandiser
- Restaurant Manager
- Animal Groomer
- Truck Driver
- Mechanic
- Warehouse Associate

Those are easy to list because it's how we've come to think about ourselves. We've been conditioned to believe that's what we *are*, but in freelancing, what you *are* doesn't matter nearly as much as what you can *do*.

Start with Tasks

Let's take one job and break it down by task to see what kind of jobs you can find as a freelancer. We'll start with an office assistant with a couple of years of experience--nothing more than a GED is required to be eligible for this position, and this person might not have even reached the age of twenty. What can he do?

- Works with Microsoft Office Suite, including Word, Excel, Powerpoint, and Outlook
- Familiar with Google Drive, including Docs, Sheets, and Presentations
- Dealing with people over the phone
- Setting appointments/working with group calendars
- Working with email
- Doing light research
- Some transcribing

This is a limited list of duties that you're probably already expanding on in your mind. When you change your focus to these kinds of things, you'll have a better idea of how the freelance world works. Most independent contractors are self-taught to some degree, leveraging their hobbies and outside interests into employment opportunities. I can't tell you how many times I've seen ads requesting personal trainers to write fitness blogs, or teachers to review or develop curriculum and study guides.

How a Client Lists a Job

Let's look at the first couple of choices a client makes when she decides to post an ad.

There are two primary types of jobs that clients advertise: short-term and long-term. The majority of the contracts you see on Upwork are short-term, but you would be surprised at how many of them turn into long-term work or extended relationships with recurring tasks. Clients themselves might just be testing the waters to see if they can find the right fit before they extend a more permanent offer. They might be startups that are unsure of what kind of work they'll have in a few weeks, but when they find a high-quality, reliable person, they'll keep reaching out as they have tasks.

Getting started

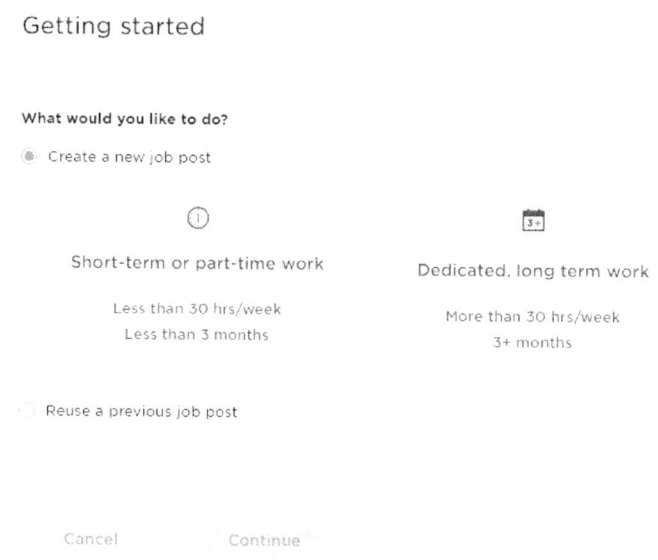

The good news is that when you're starting out, you want a series of small, short-term projects to both build up your feedback rating (more on that in a bit) and allow you to find your niche. When I began, I knew I wanted to write but had absolutely no idea what categories of freelance writing even existed. I started with resumes, not because I particularly enjoy them, but because that was the one type of writing I knew I was qualified to do. After that, I moved on to proofreading, then copywriting, blog writing, research articles, research projects, admissions essay writing (two clients in Harvard grad school so far!) editing, ghostwriting, and finally ended up as a project manager.

Freelancer Categories

There are two cool things about this: first, that you aren't limited to a box if you don't want to be. If you do find one you're comfortable in, that's awesome--you can select your niche and become an absolute expert in it. The highest-paid freelancer on Upwork charges $999 an hour and, as you can imagine, he's very specialized. The rest of us can find an interest where we might have dabbled, then bid on a beginner-level project that will allow you to test the waters and see what you can do. Is this particular task something you're interested in? Yes? Stick with it! No? Move on to the next thing.

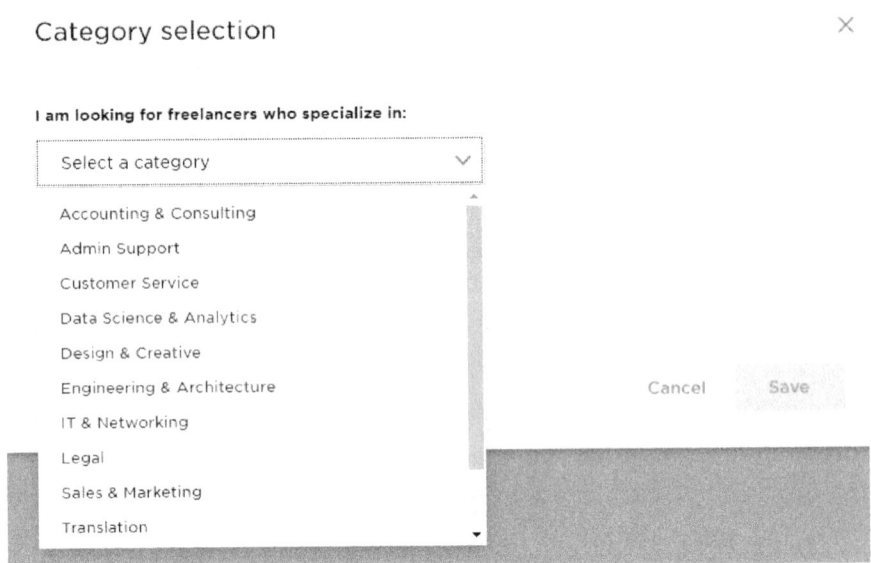

Here are the major categories of work you'll see on the platform. Each of these has a list of specialties:

Accounting & Consulting
Accounting
Bookkeeping
Business Analysis
Financial Analysis & Modeling
Financial Management/CFO

HR Administration
Instructional Design
Management Consulting
Recruiting
Tax Preparation
Training & Development

Admin Support
Data Entry
Online Research
Order Processing
Project Management
Transcription
Virtual/Administrative Assistance

Customer Service
Customer Service
Tech Support

Data Science & Analytics
A/B Testing
Bandits
Data Analytics
Data Engineering
Data Extraction
Data Mining
Data Processing
Data Visualization
Deep Learning
Experimentation & Testing
Knowledge Representation
Machine Learning

Design & Creative
2D Animation
3D Animation
Actor
Art Direction
Audio Editing/Post-Production
Audio Production
Brand Identity Design
Brand Strategy
Cartoonist
Creative Direction
Editorial Design
Exhibit Design
Fashion Design
Graphic Design
Illustration
Image Editing/Retouching
Jewelry Design
Motion Graphics Design
Music Composition
Musician
Photography
Presentation Design
Scriptwriting
Social Media Strategy
Store Design
Video Editing/Post-Production
Video Production
Videographer
Vocalist
Voice Talent
VR & AR Design

Engineering & Architecture
3D Modeling
3D Rendering
3D Visualization

Architecture
BIM Modeling
Biology
CAD
Chemical Engineering
Chemistry
Civil Engineering
Electrical Engineering
Electronic Engineering
Energy Management & Modeling
Engineering Tutoring
HVAC & MEP Design
Hydraulics Engineering
Industrial Design
Interior Design
Landscape Design
Logistics & Supply Chain Management
Mathematics
Mechanical Engineering
Oil & Gas Engineering
PCB Design
Physics
Process Engineering
Product Design
Quantity Surveying
Science Tutoring
Solar Energy
Sourcing & Procurement
Structural Engineering
Wind Energy

IT & Networking
Database Administration
DevOps Engineering
Information Security
Network Administration
Network Security
Solutions Architecture
System Administration
Systems Architecture
Systems Compliance
Systems Engineering

Legal
Business & Corporate Law
General Counsel
Immigration Law
Intellectual Property Law
International Law
Labor & Employment Law
Paralegal
Regulatory Law
Securities & Finance Law
Tax Law

Sales & Marketing
Business Development
Campaign Management
Community Management
Content Strategy
Digital Marketing
Email Marketing
Lead Generation

Market Research
Marketing Automation
Marketing Strategy
Public Relations
Search Engine Marketing
Search Engine Optimization
Social Media Marketing
Telemarketing

Translation
Language Localization
Language Tutoring
Legal Translation
Medical Translation
Technical Translation
Translation (yes, just generic translation)

Web, Mobile & Software Dev
AR/VR Development
Automation QA
Back-End Development
CMS Customization
CMS Development
Database Development
Desktop Software Development
Ecommerce Development
Emerging Tech
Firmware Development
Front-End Development
Full Stack Development
Functional QA
Game Development
Mobile App Development
Mobile Design
Mobile Game Development
Product Management
Prototyping
Scripting & Automation
Scrum Master
Software Development Tutoring
User Research
UX/UI Design
Web Design

Writing
Business Writing
Career Coaching
Content Writing
Copywriting
Creative Writing
Editing & Proofreading
Ghostwriting
Grant Writing
Technical Writing
Writing Tutoring

It really is incredible. The most accurate description of the freelancing world, and Upwork in particular, is a marketplace where you can find the number and variety of business transactions on Craigslist combined with the professionalism of LinkedIn.

One of the most exciting aspects of the freelancing world is that you can change what you do and reinvent yourself at any point. A year ago, I was working with a good buddy of mine on a freelancing project. He suddenly stopped and asked: "When people ask what you do, what do you tell them??" I laughed, because that's a great question. I typically go with writing, but I can fill a dozen different roles in a week. If you see jobs that interest you, put in a bid and branch out until you find your niche. Sometimes I have so many writing projects going that I need an escape, so I bid on research, consulting, or project management jobs just to get a break.

Other Freelancing Platforms

Although this book focuses primarily on Upwork, there are numerous other freelancing platforms. Each of these explores a slightly different niche. 99Designs, for example, is more focused on graphic design, logo creation, and anything visual. TopTal limits membership to freelancers it considers to be at the top of their fields, so if you need quality above anything else, they've already prescreened contractors for you. Here's a list of other sites you should consider exploring:

- 99Designs
- Amazon Mechanical Turk
- Broxer
- Cloud Peeps
- Codeable
- Contena
- DesignHill
- Fiverr
- FlexiJobs
- Freelance Writing
- Freelancer.com
- Guru
- HubStaff
- iWriter
- Joomlancers
- PeoplePerHour
- Programmer Meet Designer
- Remotive
- ServiceScape
- Solid Gigs
- TopTal
- You Team

Some platforms aren't designed to facilitate freelancing but can be used as such. LinkedIn and Craigslist are prime examples, and I even know contractors who primarily operate their businesses from social media platforms like Facebook, Twitter, and Instagram. I've focused on Upwork for two reasons: first, because I've found a tremendous amount of success on it as an independent contractor, and second, because I've worked with successful freelancers on that platform from virtually every industry, so I know it can work for everyone. If Upwork isn't the perfect fit for you, however, keep looking. Each of these platforms has a different approach, billing model, and clientele--and one of them is a perfect fit for you.

Upwork Freelancing Plans

Upwork offers two freelancing plans outlined in the table below. Freelancer Basic is free, while Freelancer Plus costs $14.99 per month. If you're going to be doing this part-time as supplemental income, you might want to stick with the Basic package. If you're

Basic	Plus
Free	$14.99 /month
Switch to Basic	This is your current plan
Includes:	Includes everything in Basic and also:
✓ Buy Connects as you need them for $0.15 each*	✓ 70 Connects/month
✓ Unused Connects rollover up to 140	✓ Your profile will never be set to hidden due to inactivity
✓ Hourly protection to ensure you're paid for each hour worked	✓ Setting to keep your earnings confidential
✓ Fixed-price payments are secured through milestones	✓ View competitor bids for any job
✓ Limited reports and functionality	✓ Customize your profile URL
	✓ Extended reports and functionality, including grouping and sorting

*Connects expire one year after purchase date

going to be using Upwork for any serious income, you'll want to invest in the Plus package.

Connects. The way you bid for jobs is by using "connects." These are essentially tokens, and you only get so many per month before you have to buy more. Each job requires 1 to 6 connects, depending on how valuable the contract is (i.e., longer contracts at higher values require more connects).

When I first began freelancing, I joined two platforms: Upwork and Freelancer.com. I ended up leaving the latter without ever landing a contract, and the main reason was that anyone and everyone could bid on pretty much every contract. Sometimes you'd find a job that had been posted only a few hours prior and already had 100 bids. That's *way* too many for anyone to stand out, and my time spent putting together proposals was mostly wasted.

One of the remarkable things about Upwork's business model is that they try to design everything to limit the number of contractors who see and can bid on the ad to only those who are most qualified and interested. Connects are a cornerstone of that approach. Since freelancers only have so many, it discourages contractors from shotgunning bids out for every ad that they see, and clients don't have to deal with filtering through them. You're more competitive for the jobs you're most qualified for, and it's easier for clients to find you. If you think about it, Upwork has 12 million registered freelancers, and on most jobs, you'll be competing with fewer than ten. It works.

With the Basic package, you have to purchase any connects you use at $0.15 each, sold in bundles of 10, 20, 40, 60, and 80. You can roll over up to 140 each month. With the Plus package, you get 70 free connects each month and can roll over up to 70 more unused connects, allowing you to carry a balance of up to 140. This is extremely useful: some months, you'll land large or long-term contracts and won't have to bid very much, but the next month your work might revolve around a series of small, short-term jobs. In this case, you'll enter a bidding frenzy, and having that backup store is useful. If you need more than that as a Plus member, you can also purchase connects at $0.15 each.

Since 70 connects will cost you $10.50, you're really only paying $4.49/month more for all of the other benefits of Freelancer Plus, which is why I recommend going with this plan.

Hourly protection. There are three types of contracts on Upwork: hourly, fixed-price, and retainer. The first and third in that list have you bill the client by the hour. You can manually record your hours (if the client allows that in the contract) or by using Upwork's Time Tracker. When you use the Time Tracker, Upwork will log your activity by the number of keystrokes and mouse movements you use, then periodically take screenshots of what you're doing.

This might sound a bit freaky at first, but it's for a good reason. Occasionally, things will go south with a client. It doesn't happen often, but you might have a client who argues that you didn't do the work he requested and refuses to pay, or who suddenly runs out of money after you've billed 30 hours of work in a week. If something like this happens and you've used the Time Tracker, an Upwork specialist will review your work diary. When they confirm that you did, in fact, spend the time you billed actively working on the contract, then Upwork guarantees your payment. They'll send you the money upfront and take on the responsibility of pursuing reimbursement from the client. If you bill hours manually, however, you don't have this protection. This feature applies to both Upwork freelancer packages.

Fixed-price milestones. The other type of contract I mentioned was fixed-price. Sometimes it's easier to set up work per the product delivered; for example, if you're a graphic designer and a client wants you to design twenty ad banners at a set price for each one. These contracts are set up around milestones for a given amount of work (e.g., one ad banner). The client has to fund these milestones by depositing the amount you've agreed upon with Upwork before you begin the work. Again, you'll occasionally (it's pretty rare, but it does happen) encounter a client who doesn't want to pay for the work you've delivered. If that happens, an Upwork specialist will review what's happened and the work you've submitted; he can approve payment if the client is unreasonable. This feature applies to both Upwork freelancer packages.

Reports & functionality. Upwork Basic includes everything you need to use the platform, so there aren't any "must-haves" that you'll be missing with the free package. That being said, Upwork makes a number of reports and features available to Upwork Plus members that can drastically simplify some of the admin aspects of freelancing. This can be very useful, especially when tax season rolls around.

Hidden/private profiles. There are three visibility settings for your profile: Public, Only Upwork Users, and Private. Public allows you to be found on the platform and externally, which can be really good for business. I've had several clients Google me, then contact me via LinkedIn or Facebook. I later found out that they'd glanced at my profile from the results they found on Google.

When your profile is set to Only Upwork Users, you're not shown to external search engines and can only be found by clients on the Upwork platform. There are various personal reasons for this; perhaps you're in an industry where moonlighting on the side isn't prohibited, but it's frowned upon. This setting prevents someone from finding you unless they're on Upwork as well.

The Private setting hides you from all searches, both on and off the platform. You can voluntarily switch to this if you know you won't be active for a while. You won't be invited to any jobs, which means you won't get dinged for not responding. If you're an Upwork Basic freelancer, your profile will automatically be set to Private if one of two things happens:

1. You don't submit a proposal within 90 days of joining.
2. You don't earn money within 90 days of submitting your first proposal.

Upwork only wants active freelancers on the platform, so you have to be bidding, and you have to win at least one of those bids within three months. If you're a Plus member, those timelines are extended out to two years.

Confidential earnings. The default setting on your profile shows what contracts you've had and how much you earned. When you're an Upwork Plus member, you can set your earnings to private. The contracts and feedback will still be shown, but the amount you earned on each one will be hidden.

There are a few reasons why you might want to do this. If you've experienced a sudden jump in qualifications or skills and increased your pay accordingly, it might be good to hide your earnings for a while. Let's say you started on Upwork as a paralegal while you were going to law school, but recently graduated, passed the bar, and want to begin charging fees worthy of a practicing attorney. You don't want your history of jobs at $15 an hour to work against you when you're now bidding at $75 an hour. Wait until you've closed out four or five contracts at your higher rate of pay, then make your earnings public again.

Perhaps you've established yourself on Upwork as a part-time freelancer, and all twenty contracts you've closed so far have been fixed-price, short-term jobs. You've decided to make the jump into full-time independent contracting and are bidding on larger, longer-term positions. If you suspect that clients would be turned off by seeing that you've only worked small jobs before, you can hide your earnings until you've landed a few long-term contracts.

Finally, some people are just uncomfortable with having their earnings displayed. While this is understandable, it's something I would challenge you to work on for two reasons. First, your profile is your new resume, and it's the lion's share of how potential clients evaluate you. Being able to back up what you're charging with a history of completed contracts and satisfied clients significantly bolsters your chances of continuing charging that rate. Second, aligning yourself with the culture of an organization is a critical aspect of success. The vast majority of Upwork freelancers don't hide their earnings, so hiding something that all of your competition makes public could negatively affect your chances of winning jobs.

Viewing competitor bids. This is, by far, the feature of Upwork Plus that I use most frequently, and it's incredibly useful if you're just starting your freelancing journey. When you open a job posting as an Upwork Plus member, you can see the highest quote, the lowest quote, and the average of all of the bids. Below are examples of hourly and fixed-price bid ranges.

Bid range - **High $80.00 | Avg $60.83 | Low $45.00**
Bid range - **High $14,500.00 | Avg $6,194.45 | Low $2,000.00**

One of the most common challenges for beginners is knowing what to charge. Because an employer is gaining so many advantages by hiring an independent contractor, they can afford to pay substantially more. Even if you know that you'd charge $25 an hour for a particular task as part of a "normal" job, doing that as a freelancer might net you $37 an hour. If you're trying to figure out what you should charge from scratch, it gets even more complicated. As you explore your skills and work with various products or services, being able to see high, low, and average bid ranges is incredibly useful.

If you're an experienced freelancer, this can help you be more profitable and more efficient. I've won several jobs where my profile rate was set $20 to $30 an hour lower than the average quote. I increased my bid to that level, won the job, and saw a healthy increase in profit simply by having access to this data. The flip side makes you more efficient: if you see a job that would be a good fit for your skills, but it's going for $20 to $30 less than you'd like to bid, don't waste your time. Keep looking for contracts within your price range.

Customized URL. This is a branding feature that can be useful if you refer outside clients to your Upwork profile. If you're an established freelancer and are just joining the platform, I highly recommend taking advantage of this. In Chapter Five, I'll show you how to bring non-Upwork clients onto the platform both cheaply and simply, giving you the benefits and protections the platform provides at a discounted rate.

Expanded reports & functionality. As an Upwork Plus member, you'll gain access to admin tools that simplify working the back end of independent contracting. This is particularly useful when it comes time to file taxes. It's also handy if you have multiple streams of income: you can separate your Upwork clients from non-Upwork labor.

One of the things you'll find as you begin your Upwork career is that the platform doesn't do a tremendous amount to support beginning freelancers. While that isn't a fun place to be, it's understandable. It's hit or miss whether a contractor will stay on the platform, and creating labor-intensive processes to walk you through different aspects of learning the platform isn't cost-effective for them. That's why this book is so essential!

The good news is that once you become an established freelancer, and particularly once you earn the Top Rated or higher badges, the level of service increases exponentially. Chat support, quick responses, and a tremendous amount of help are available at your fingertips. You've got to put in the effort to show that you're committed; once you do, Upwork is all about making you successful.

Chapter One Exercise

Open up a blank document and write out twenty things you can do. These can be minor tasks (e.g., "PowerPoint," "typing," "answering phones") or duties in previous jobs (e.g., "managing a shared calendar," "overseeing a hiring process"). They could be hobbies (such as fishing, knitting, or reading) or interests you've explored (like travel, trying new coffee shops, or taking every personality test on Facebook). Pause here and come back when you have twenty items on your sheet.

The second part of this exercise is to work through the Freelancer Categories listed in this chapter. Compare them to your list and see how many you can find.

A friend I grew up with loved to do accents and impersonations; he's now a full-time freelancer who works as a voice actor and has had several commercials appear on national TV. Another tried keto out with his girlfriend; they were so happy with it that they launched a recipe site, and now they're well-recognized experts in that field with two keto books in the "For Dummies" series. Don't be intimidated by having to define what you can do--it's a natural reaction, but you need to fight it. If you have a work history, hobbies, and interests, I guarantee you have skills that can translate into independent contracting.

Chapter Two

Anatomy of an Ad

Note: If you purchased my Freelancing Foundations book, you'll recognize this section. I chose to put this in both books because it's so critical. Even if you've read it before or have been on Upwork for years, I highly recommend perusing this section again. Small tweaks in your contract search and evaluation strategy can revolutionize your work life.

One of the ways to find your niche is to look at what's being posted. Let's take a few minutes to work through the job search function on Upwork. While this might seem somewhat elementary, don't skip this part. The search function is not only how freelancers find jobs, but it's also how clients find freelancers. The more you can assimilate yourself into the Upwork subculture, the better you'll be able to use those tools to describe and position yourself.

Optimizing Your Job Feed

On the left side of the page, you'll find an area titled "My Categories." If this is your first time logging into the site, it will likely be empty. Take a moment to click on the pen icon and explore the list of categories. You can select up to ten: the more you choose, the more potential jobs will appear in your feed. You can adjust these at any time, so if you're not seeing the kinds of jobs that appeal to you, continually edit this section until the type of work you're interested in consistently appears.

Once you join a talent cloud (I'll discuss this in detail in Chapter Three), a hyperlinked quick search will appear on the left side menu. This will allow you to rapidly review your talent clouds and see if any new jobs have been posted. The final section on this left margin is for your saved searches. We're about to review the available filters; once you've found a search that matches you with the kind of ads you're looking for, save it, so you don't have to remember and re-enter all of the settings next time.

Using Filtered Search

Using the Filtered Search function allows you to search for extremely precise criteria. If you're trying to find one specific job, go here first. However, if you're just trying to cast a broad net, you'll need to click the green magnifying glass button next to the search bar. This will technically conduct a search (even if you haven't entered any text), and the next screen gives you the ability to employ filters.

PRO TIP

"Filtered Search" is different than "Advanced Search." "Advanced" gives you options to find one extremely specific job post. "Filtered" lets you find the type of jobs you want.

I'm completely confident in your ability to read and use common sense to figure out what each filter does--but don't skip reading this section. Each of these filters has a strategy to it: understanding what each filter *does* is different than understanding what it *means* for you as a contractor.

Job type. There are three types of jobs on Upwork: Hourly, Fixed Price, and Retainer. Depending on the industry, you'll find a prevalence of one over the other. As a writer, most of my work tends to be fixed price. When I put on my editor or project manager hats, however, the jobs tend to be hourly. Retainers tend to be geared more toward highly specialized skill sets such as legal advice, HR consulting, or marketing feedback. None of these is better than the others, but each comes with considerations.

Fixed price jobs can be broken up into milestones, so if you've got a large, thousand-dollar project that might take a couple of weeks, you don't have to wait until the very end to receive anything. You'll negotiate any milestones and due dates with each client.

Hourly jobs are tracked in one of two ways: you can either do it manually, or you can use Upwork's Time Tracker, a downloadable app that tracks your time per contract by recording the total number of keystrokes, mouse movements, and taking screenshots at random times. Using the time tracker makes you eligible for Upwork's Payment Protection, which means that even if something goes wrong with finances on the client's side (or they refuse to pay), Upwork will pay you for those hours. Manually recording hours is easier for you, but since it lends itself to overbilling (which I've seen from the client side on multiple occasions), it isn't eligible for Payment Protection. Clients also have to authorize manual time, so if you work on hourly jobs to any degree, you'll eventually have to use the time tracker. Neither method is better, but you should understand the differences between them.

Finally, retainer jobs are offered when a client might need occasional advice and won't have time to look for a new expert for every task. They pay a weekly base rate to retain the contractor, then any actual work is billed at an hourly rate. This can be useful for a small business that will need occasional work from someone with a specific skill set but isn't required every week.

My buddy, the one who got me on Upwork, prefers fixed-price jobs to hourly rates for several personal reasons. There's nothing wrong with that, and you might find yourself in the same boat. However, you need to seek out hourly jobs until you log 101 hours. When a client creates a job posting, he can mark down selection criteria--one of them is to limit the job to contractors who have recorded more than 100 hours on Upwork. Ironically, this is available even if the job being posted is a fixed price job. It's a general mark of experience, so make sure that this is one of your eventual goals.

Experience level. Many people are tempted to overestimate their experience or qualifications here, assuming that saying they're an "expert" makes it more likely that they'll get the job. This is wrong for several reasons. First, there's no universally defined standard for each experience level. This is a selection the client makes on the job post itself to help the right freelancers find it, but anyone can apply for jobs at any experience level.

Because these describe job posts and not freelancers, how you classify yourself is mostly in your mind. As you start your freelancing career, it's better to default to assuming you're slightly less qualified than you are. Bidding on lower-level jobs with an (actual) higher experience level will make it easier for you to win the bid, even if you have less recorded experience on the platform. It will also make it easier to knock the job out of the park, performance-wise, and what you're going for in your first ten contracts are high ratings. Establishing a solid feedback rating and client history will make all of the difference in your long-term success on any particular platform.

Client history. You want clients to have a history for the same reason they want you to have it: you want to know what you're getting into. Clients who are posting jobs on Upwork for the first time are a bit risky: they don't have any allegiance to the platform, and I've seen more than a few post a job ad and never log in again. You don't want to waste time, energy, and connects applying for a job that won't be realized. At the same time, some of the best clients I've had have been first-timers. Don't discriminate heavily here, but be cautious with this demographic.

Clients with five or more hires tend to be pretty committed to using Upwork, so if they post an ad, they're likely going to hire. Once someone has hired five or more freelancers, they know what they're doing, they like what they see on Upwork, and they're likely going to be good clients. I've been extremely impressed by the quality of clients Upwork attracts and retains. Out of the hundred contracts I've worked, I've only had negative experiences with a few of them. More often than not, they were newcomers to the site. If someone has been around for a while and is still hiring, the odds are high that you can expect a pleasant, professional working relationship.

Client info. This is a bit of a catch-all category with disparate filters. If clients you've previously worked with have an active ad, you can filter to find those. I always try to maintain good relationships with my clients, and one of the advantages can be found here. If you do quality work for someone and then apply for another job they post later, you've already got a foot in the door. I've been hired for several contracts simply because the client remembered me and bumped me to the top of the list.

When you first join Upwork as a client, you can provide and verify a payment mechanism (typically a credit or debit card). Clients who have not verified a payment method are far less likely to stick around--they're doing the equivalent of posting a job on Craigslist and seeing what happens. If they're blown away by a candidate quickly, they might hire--if they don't find what they're looking for rapidly, those odds go down sharply. Similar to client history, this isn't a reason *not* to bid on a job; I've had some fantastic first-time clients. However, there is a higher-than-normal chance that they won't hire on the platform. There's a psychological commitment that comes when someone enters their credit card information, so if someone has verified their payment, the chances they'll hire are higher.

Number of proposals. I have two guidelines that go hand in hand here. The first is that I generally don't apply for any jobs with more than ten applicants already, and I rarely consider ads that have been posted for longer than 24 hours. Bidding is a necessary part of freelancing, but it takes time, you don't get paid for it, and you have to pay for the connects that are required to submit a bid. I try to maximize the value of each work hour by only bidding on jobs I have a fair chance of winning, and I've found that once more than ten freelancers have submitted bids, it gets much more difficult to distinguish yourself from the pack. Upwork advertises that it takes an average of 72 hours to fill a job post; in my experience, this is roughly what happens:

- First 24 hours: Bids are solicited.
- Second 24 hours: The client picks the freelancers she wants to interview and opens discussion channels with them.
- Third 24 hours: Details are finalized, and the contract is awarded.

By the second day, the client has found qualified contractors and has already started the interview process. Even if she gets additional bids at this point, she's not likely to give them an in-depth look--if she checks them out at all. It's still possible to get the job, but it isn't common.

Budget. I generally recommend avoiding this filter altogether. It isn't uncommon for clients to use placeholder values (e.g., $5) and tell you to bid what you think it will cost--and sometimes these can be pretty substantial jobs. If you eliminate all the $5 ads, you'll miss these altogether. Some of the most lucrative, long-term jobs are posted like this because the client wants your help defining the scope of work, outlining milestones, and determining the overall budget. The average amount I've been paid for ads listed at $5 ends up being closer to $1,000.

That being said, you really need to be comfortable with your fixed-price estimates before helping a client define the scope of work. If you and she agree on a price and you end up losing money, you have two choices. You can either eat it and not complain (which no one likes to do) or request additional payments. Clients generally aren't happy when someone quotes work, wins a bid, then comes back later and raises the price. Bidding accurately is vital.

Hours per week. This filter applies exclusively to hourly jobs. The vast majority of the time, clients are estimating the amount of time it will take to complete a job, and they're being found by freelancers who are calculating how much time they have available. The more experience both sides have, the more accurate this will be. If you're just getting started and working with a relatively new client, this can vary broadly.

I have a whiteboard in my office where I list all of the work I have going on this week and all of the work I have projected for next week. Next to each fixed-price job, I estimate the number of hours I think it will take, then use that to determine what contracts I bid for.

Project length. This is, again, a relative indicator. Short-term jobs can often turn into long-term employment, and I've had contracts cut short when the client's scope of work changes. In my experience, this is two-thirds accurate; the other third changes to some degree afterward. Generally, it ends up with subsequent tasks, which is always what you want to see. Only occasionally have I had clients significantly shorten the work they wanted to be done.

When you're first starting, it helps to get an idea of what jobs are available and how they're listed. As with any environment, Upwork has a unique culture that might be different than your expectations. Perhaps clients list work in different categories than you would expect. One of the most common adjustments I see involves clients who advertise jobs at a certain level but offer significantly less than what you'll see for the same work elsewhere on the platform. For example, fixed-price writing jobs *generally* roll with 5 cents or less per word for entry-level writers, 7 to 10 cents per word for intermediate-level writers, and 15 cents or more for the highest quality. This can, of course, vary considerably based on many factors, but it's always amusing to me when clients post work they list as expert level and then offer 2 cents per word.

Exploring what's available is also useful to help calibrate what you should be charging for your services. If you have Upwork Plus (covered at the end of Chapter One), you'll get a window into the bid range by seeing the amount of the highest bid, the value of the lowest, and the average of all of the quotes. Perusing the last week's worth of jobs in any given category will provide tremendous insight into what the going rate for a particular task is.

What a Freelancer Sees

Now that you have a general idea of what's available, let's dig a bit deeper into a job posting itself.

The first thing you notice about the job post is the headline. Don't be afraid to open up ads that appear to be outside of your comfort zone--clients create their own headlines, and occasionally you'll find one that's been rather severely mislabeled and falls into your skillset.

Beneath the headline is the job category hyperlink: this tells you how the client classified the overall job. If you want to find more like it, simply

Anatomy of an Ad

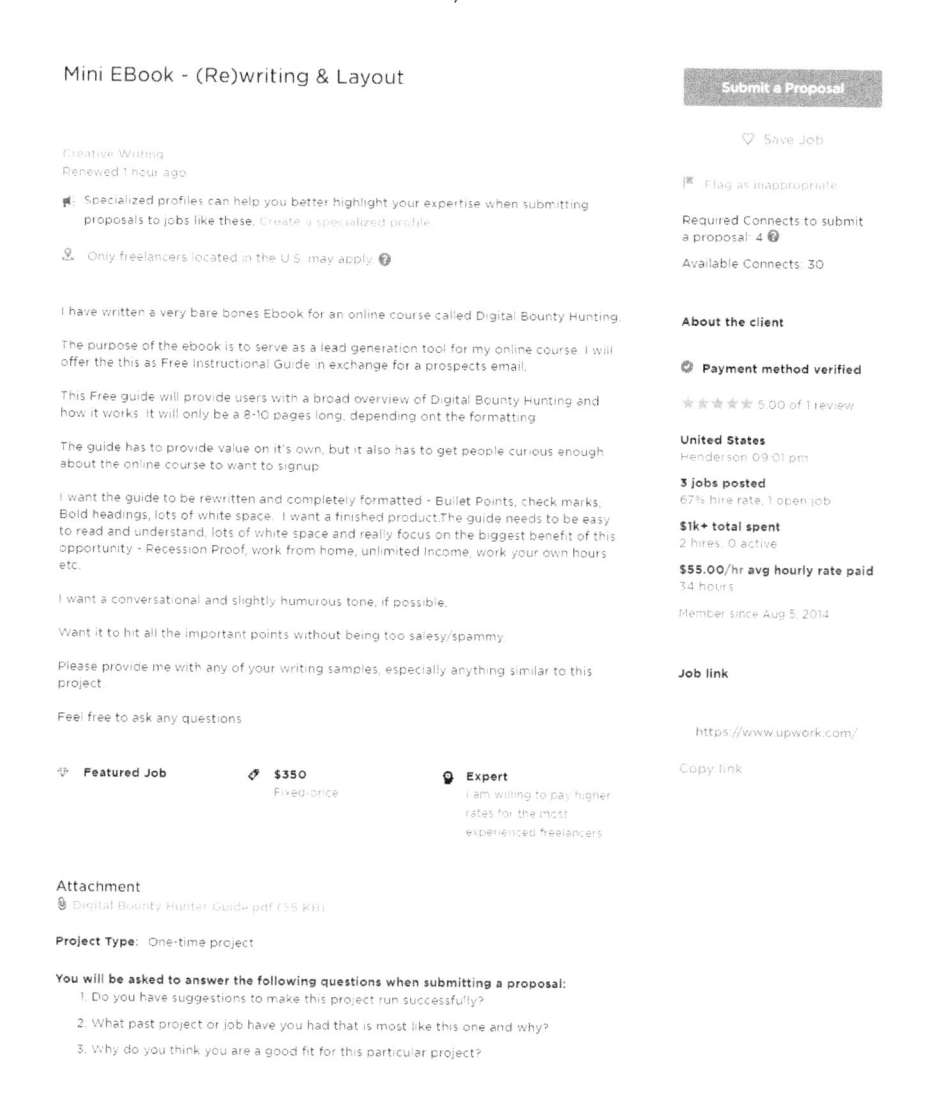

Mini EBook - (Re)writing & Layout

Creative Writing
Renewed 1 hour ago

- Specialized profiles can help you better highlight your expertise when submitting proposals to jobs like these. Create a specialized profile.

- Only freelancers located in the U.S. may apply.

I have written a very bare bones Ebook for an online course called Digital Bounty Hunting.

The purpose of the ebook is to serve as a lead generation tool for my online course. I will offer the this as Free Instructional Guide in exchange for a prospects email.

This Free guide will provide users with a broad overview of Digital Bounty Hunting and how it works. It will only be a 8-10 pages long, depending ont the formatting.

The guide has to provide value on it's own, but it also has to get people curious enough about the online course to want to signup.

I want the guide to be rewritten and completely formatted - Bullet Points, check marks, Bold headings, lots of white space. I want a finished product.The guide needs to be easy to read and understand, lots of white space and really focus on the biggest benefit of this opportunity - Recession Proof, work from home, unlimited Income, work your own hours etc.

I want a conversational and slightly humurous tone, if possible.

Want it to hit all the important points without being too salesy/spammy

Please provide me with any of your writing samples, especially anything similar to this project.

Feel free to ask any questions

- Featured Job
- $350 Fixed-price
- Expert — I am willing to pay higher rates for the most experienced freelancers

Attachment
Digital Bounty Hunter Guide.pdf (55 KB)

Project Type: One-time project

You will be asked to answer the following questions when submitting a proposal:
1. Do you have suggestions to make this project run successfully?
2. What past project or job have you had that is most like this one and why?
3. Why do you think you are a good fit for this particular project?

Submit a Proposal

♡ Save Job

⚑ Flag as inappropriate

Required Connects to submit a proposal: 4
Available Connects: 30

About the client

✓ Payment method verified

★★★★★ 5.00 of 1 review

United States
Henderson 09:01 pm

3 jobs posted
67% hire rate, 1 open job

$1k+ total spent
2 hires, 0 active

$55.00/hr avg hourly rate paid
34 hours

Member since Aug 5, 2014

Job link

https://www.upwork.com/

Copy link

---

click on the text that reads "Creative Writing" and a new window will open with all of the ads for which you're qualified in that genre.

In addition to job types, clients can restrict ads by location in two primary ways. The first is by indicating that only freelancers who are located in the United States may apply. The majority of Upwork traffic comes from American clients, and depending on the project, they might need someone with an understanding of all the subtle nuances of American culture. You can't apply for these jobs unless Upwork has verified your location within the States.

The second location restriction is by city or time zone. If a client, for example, wants to hire a virtual assistant or someone to make sales calls, she might indicate a preference for contractors in the Eastern Daylight Time zone. If that's the case, it will be marked in the "Preferred Qualifications" at the bottom of the ad. You'll find quite a bit of information here. Clients can indicate several preferred qualifications: Upwork success level based on Job Success Score (JSS), language proficiency, experience level, advertised pay rate, among others. Unlike the "U.S. Only" indicator they made at the top, none of these criteria will prevent you from bidding for them. Keep in mind that Upwork will highlight any mismatches for the client--if you want to win the bid, you need to be prepared to justify why she should adjust her preferences to hire you. Sometimes these are hard and fast requirements, and sometimes they're just preferences. Occasionally, clients will simply click these options without understanding what they are, and they don't have any actual preferences at all.

Each of these qualifications serves as a filter for clients to proactively find freelancers. You want to be seen by clients for several reasons. You'll be exposed to jobs you might not find on your own, you automatically get selected for an interview if you respond, and you don't have to pay for any connects when you apply to jobs to which you've been invited. The jobs are also generally preselected for your skill sets, making it easier to find work than if you had to go out and wade through all of the posts you don't want to see. In Chapter Three, I'll walk through each indicator on your profile and explain how these impact Upwork freelancer searches and the bidding process as a whole.

You can also see what kind of activity there's been on the job. Upwork advertises that it takes clients an average of 72 hours to hire someone, so these indicators are invaluable. "Proposals" shows how many freelancers have bid on the job. If the client has shown interest in a particular contractor and messaged him or her, that will show in the "Interviewing" number. Clients are prompted to proactively invite freelancers to their job posting, although this isn't required. If they've done this, you can see this reflected in the next two sections: the total number of invites sent, and the number of invited freelancers who haven't responded yet. Invited freelancers who have responded automatically get included in the "Interviewing" category.

When a client receives a bid that he knows he won't hire, he can do one of two things. He can ignore it, which is what most people do, or he can archive it. When a bid is archived, it's removed from the "Proposals" number. A client could have received 100 bids and archived 95 of them; in this case, the "Proposals" number on the job ad would only show five.

The section above Qualifications and Activity is about Skills and Expertise. You can glean some information from here, particularly if the client is unclear in his job description. As a general rule, you won't review this section often, though--it primarily lists categories Upwork uses for search filters and won't affect you otherwise.

Above that, you'll find a section with three main features: attachments, project type, and additional questions. Clients can attach files to their job posting, and it's helpful to open these and have a look. They'll likely explain the significance of each file in the ad, and these give quite a bit of context for what the project will probably require. Always open these and at least glance through them.

Screening questions are something I'm not a fan of, but they have a purpose. Clients can choose from a pre-populated list of standard queries, or they can write their own. I don't like them because clients often use them because they seem like a good idea; once they start working through the proposals, it ends up being so much additional reading that it isn't uncommon for them to skip past all of the responses. You're required to answer all of the screening questions when submitting a bid, and it can eat up a substantial amount of time. However, the silver lining is that screening questions can separate freelancers who legitimately want that project from those who are shotgunning bids and looking for any available work. I'll show you what you should (and shouldn't) write here when we get to Chapter Five.

Connects. These are essentially tokens that allow you to bid for jobs. I explain this in-depth in Chapter One. Bidding for a job requires 1 to 6 connects, depending on the advertised value. Contracts that are long-term or highly-priced require more connects, while short-term and cheaper posts require fewer. If you're invited to interview for a job, however, you aren't charged any connects. These are free applications, so always respond to invitations ASAP.

Saving jobs. You can "save" a job by clicking on the green heart in the upper right-hand corner. Because you want to bid on jobs quickly, I recommend using this in only two ways. First, it isn't uncommon for me to scroll through and find jobs on my phone, but I only ever submit bids from my computer. I'll work through my feed or search results and save all of the posts I'm interested in; when I get back to my computer, I'll pull up my Saved Jobs list (found under the "FIND WORK" tab at the top of your home screen) and then apply to them.

The other reason I save jobs is for market research. I'll have you conduct a series of exercises in this book, and this will be a valuable feature as you work through them. Sometimes I'm considering expanding into a particular field by developing a new skill set--let's say I'm interested in search engine optimization (SEO), but I'm not sure how much those jobs are worth. As I find these, I'll save them, then go back a few days later once the contract has been awarded and check out how much competition there was and get an idea for the typical bid ranges.

Flagging as inappropriate. Although Upwork does a great job of filtering clients and creating an ad process that prevents spam, you'll sometimes see problems slip through the cracks. Before I get into the specific reasons for flagging, I want to address something more foundational that will (hopefully) shape your perspective on this issue.

Upwork is a community. After years of working with over a hundred clients and nearly a thousand other freelancers, I can confidently say that what's good for the community is good for you. Even encouraging high-quality competitors with my precise skill sets in my specific field to join is good for me. It cements Upwork's reputation as a place you go to find quality writers, increasing the number of clients and job opportunities available to me. Since neither I nor my direct competition can handle all of the work, I find that there's enough to go around.

I've seen people get stuck in an overly competitive mindset where they want to leave problems up to distract their competition, assuming it will give them a competitive edge. Perhaps they find a spam ad and don't flag it, hoping it will suck their competition in and make other jobs less competitive. This is the wrong attitude, and it hurts you in the long run. If you find a client who is offering to pay you outside of Upwork, they're going to continue to do that--and that will prevent you from having access to those future opportunities.

There's a business concept known as "Blue Ocean Strategy." It's based on a fishing analogy and compares two mindsets: someone who fishes in a pond and another who fishes in the ocean. The person who focuses on a small body of water knows that only so many

> **Flag as inappropriate**   ✕
>
> ○ Client is offering payment outside of Upwork
> ○ Person is attempting to buy or use my Upwork account
> ○ Client is misrepresenting their identity
> ○ Job post looks like a scam or contains a suspicious link
> ○ Job post contains contact information
> ○ It's something else
>
> Additional details
>
>   Cancel   **Submit**

fish are available, so he'll zealously guard his coveted spot to keep anyone from discovering it. This represents niche occupational fields where there are only so many clients. Conversely, a blue ocean mindset believes that there are enough fish for everyone; what's most important is taking care of the ocean itself. Remember, what's good for the community is good for you.

There are five standardized reasons why an ad should be flagged, plus a "catch-all" option for anything else you find suspicious. The first and fifth reasons are similar; these clients are trying to use Upwork as a job board and then hire outside the platform. If you do this, not only are you violating Upwork's terms and conditions (endangering your future on this very profitable site), you're also giving up all of the protections Upwork provides freelancers. As a career independent contractor, I can tell you that these are worth it.

Although I've never personally encountered the second or third reasons, I could see why someone would do this. Upwork is a feedback-intensive system, and this is used to weed out subpar contractors and clients. If someone has destroyed their reputation, they might consider hiring someone else to continue to get work or hide their own identity to continue to use the platform. Don't go along with these. Remember, the only reasons for these revolve around them being untrustworthy, so no matter what they offer you, turn it down.

If you see a job that looks spammy, flag it. Clients will occasionally reference external information, such as including the link to their site to demonstrate some aspect of the work they want to be completed. Other than obviously legitimate reasons like this, if it feels suspicious, it probably is. Authentic clients should never ask for personally identifiable information or for you to complete a job application outside of Upwork.

Finally, use the catch-all when you see something that you feel goes against the good of the platform. I've used this a couple of times to flag ads with discriminatory hiring practices. For example, hiring someone **familiar** with a particular religion is fine, but advertising that they have to be **a member of** that religion is discriminatory.

About the client. You'll find seven pieces of data in the "About the client" section. This is covered in more detail in Chapter Four, but I'll briefly summarize it here. The first is whether their method of payment has been verified. Whenever someone is serious about hiring or has already hired, they're required to connect a credit card or bank account to their Upwork client account. If they've done this, you know they're a serious client. If they haven't, they're not committed. They might hire someone, of course, but the chances go down substantially. I nearly always avoid submitting bids for clients who haven't verified a payment method.

Next, you'll see their reviews based on a five-star system. These work just as you'd see on Amazon products: the higher the average and the more ratings they've received, the better of a client they are.

About the client

Upwork Enterprise Client

✅ **Payment method verified**

Indeed

⭐⭐⭐⭐⭐
4.97 of 5891 reviews

United States
Stamford 08:43 am

2779 jobs posted
93% hire rate, 5 open jobs

$10M+ total spent
9,982 hires, 404 active

$10.04/hr avg hourly rate paid
474,929 hours

Member since Feb 22, 2017

For example, this is Indeed.com's client profile. I've worked with them extensively and can validate that they've earned their rating:

When you've got a 4.97 average across nearly 6,000 reviews, you're a quality client--period.

After that is the client's location. This is mostly irrelevant as a hiring factor since the vast majority of jobs can be completed from virtually anywhere. However, this can help establish a personal rapport with a client if you're familiar with the area and can mention something about it in your cover letter.

You can see the number of jobs they've posted, their hiring rate, and how many jobs they currently have open. This gives you an idea of how active that client is. In the Indeed example above, they've averaged three job posts per day, seven days a week, for the last two and a half years. They also have one of the highest hiring rates I've seen at 93 percent. The hiring rate is determined by whether they hire for a job they post or not. Low rates indicate that either they can't find the talent they're looking for, they're fishing, or they're flaky. Anything above 50 percent is considered stable, but if you see a client lower than that, be wary.

How much money they've spent just demonstrates their commitment to using Upwork. There's no set standard you should look for, but over time you'll develop a feel for what this should look like compared to other elements, such as the number of freelancers they've hired.

The average hourly rate can be intimidating if you're looking at a client that hires globally. Remember that extremely qualified talent can be found in the Philippines or India for $5 - $10 an hour in many industries. If the client has worked with international contractors, it will decrease their average hourly rate, but this doesn't necessarily mean that's the amount they'll be looking to pay US contractors.

Finally, you can see how long a client has been on Upwork. Again, there's no hard and fast rule regarding what you should look for here, but it's another data point that can indicate how committed a client is to using the platform.

Similar jobs on Upwork. At the bottom of an ad, you'll often find a section that lists similar jobs. This can be very useful if you find a contract that advertises the type of work you prefer, but you don't want to submit a bid for this particular job because of the warning signs you've seen in other areas that I just covered. Clicking on these will lead you to other opportunities that might be a better fit.

This is also useful if you're researching a skill set you want to develop or an area you're considering bidding for. You can quickly get a good idea of the type of work available, how much it pays, and what kind of clients are advertising in this category.

What a Client Sees

When a client creates a job posting, he'll select a category and subcategory. This doesn't limit who can apply for it; Upwork uses this information to advertise the job to the right freelancers. We'll come back to this when we walk through a profile and how to optimize it to attract clients.

The next set of fields classifies what type of job, task, or project the client is advertising. One-time projects often have a way of translating to continued opportunities if you do a great job, so never underestimate the importance of overdelivering and maintaining excellent client relationships. One of the principles I discovered was that investing in client satisfaction needs to be an absolute priority--this has done more for my freelancing career than anything else.

One of my early clients hired me to write occasional blog posts about a diet I'd never tried. Within a few months, he asked me to take on the role of an editor and lead a news team, where I've supervised more than two dozen writers and a graphic designer. Eventually, this led to a ghostwriting opportunity, and we published two books together. That client is a lifelong friend at this point, and going to work with only people you'd sit down and have a beer with adds tremendous value to your work/life balance.

Even if clients have a long-term position in mind, it isn't uncommon to post the job as a short-term, smaller project. Finding the right fit is critical, and it's easier to do that with a task that has limited scope than advertising a full-time job right off the bat. However, if they do this, they'll also want to find someone open to long-term work and expanded responsibilities. They'll usually mention that in the description.

There are three project types: one-time, ongoing, and complex. The first type is usually a smaller job, although it can be a sizeable standalone project. These are tasks like writing a single paper, designing a small batch of images as a graphic designer, or updating a website. Clients commonly follow up with more work for freelancers who do well, so make sure you put your best effort into each contract. You'll apply a well-known lesson from business school here: it's much easier to retain a customer than it is to gain a new one.

Details
Step 3 of 8

What type of project do you have?

One-time project
Find the right skills for a short-term need.

Ongoing project
Find a skilled resource for an extended engagement.

Complex project
Find specialized experts and agencies for large projects.

Clients will often include screening questions to ask about a particular aspect of the job. These are added below the field for a cover letter and must be answered to submit a bid. This is an excellent tool for the client to weed out unqualified freelancers, and it's a perfect area to stand out if you've got what they're looking for. See Chapter Five, "Placing a Winning Bid," for an in-depth discussion of what these are and what kind of responses you should give (as a freelancer) and expect (as a client).

A client can customize the job profile by selecting specific skills or areas of expertise essential for the position. For example, here are the ones I've chosen for my virtual assistant:

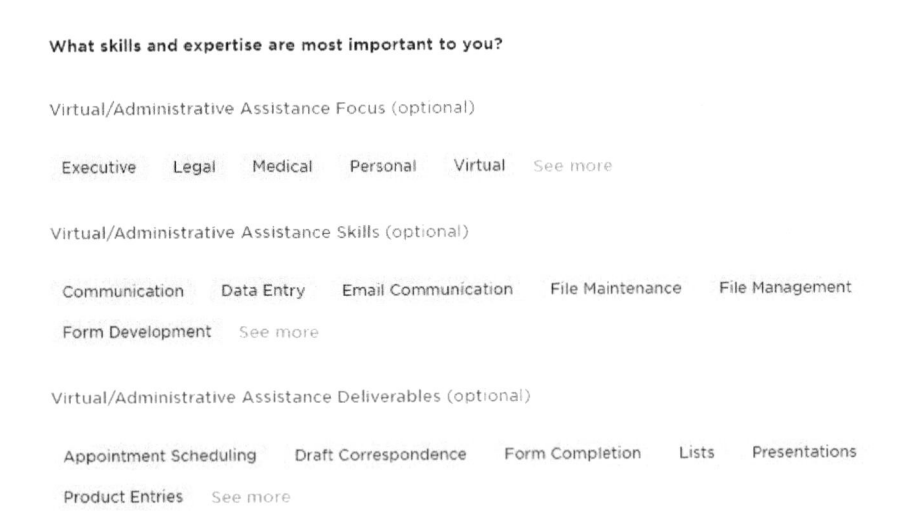

What skills and expertise are most important to you?

Virtual/Administrative Assistance Focus (optional)

Executive   Legal   Medical   Personal   Virtual   See more

Virtual/Administrative Assistance Skills (optional)

Communication   Data Entry   Email Communication   File Maintenance   File Management
Form Development   See more

Virtual/Administrative Assistance Deliverables (optional)

Appointment Scheduling   Draft Correspondence   Form Completion   Lists   Presentations
Product Entries   See more

As you can imagine, clients often have different "soft" requirements for specific jobs, such as fluency with a particular language. A client can specify hundreds of skills and expertise, creating a unique combination that clearly communicates what he is looking for. Alternately, I've seen job ads with very few requirements. None of these are fixed, but they can be indicators of the type of work you can expect.

The majority of work available on Upwork can be performed virtually, but certain types of jobs require a specific geographic location. This starts at the national level--a client can specify whether he'll consider clients only within the United States or anywhere in the world. Contracts posted for US-only freelancers tend to have 75 percent higher rates, 50 percent larger contract size, and 20 percent less competition. If you're in the States, you'll want to make sure you can search for these, and you do that by selecting the "U.S. Only" tab on the left side of your job feed. If that option isn't available to you, it's because you haven't confirmed your location yet. If you're not in the States, consider working with an agency that can give you access to a lot of those lucrative contracts.

Clients can be selective. I've had four clients find me on LinkedIn or Facebook, interview me there, then create a client profile on Upwork just to hire me. Once that happens, they create a job posting that is invite-only, then send me a link.

If clients find you outside of Upwork, you're not required to bring them onto the platform. However, you might want to consider it. Upwork offers numerous benefits to freelancers, foremost of which is handling payment details. A client will deposit the money into escrow with Upwork, which means it will be released much more quickly, and you don't have to worry about billing or follow-up. If you find clients on Upwork, you'll initially surrender 20 percent of your earnings as a commission to the platform, then 10 percent, finally arriving at 5 percent (depending on several factors covered in Chapter Four). However, if you bring clients onto the platform, you only pay 3.4 percent, and that amount is worth it to me not to worry about anything billing-related. This is covered in Chapter Five.

It isn't uncommon to see a job posting that needs more than one freelancer, so don't be discouraged if you're not first in line. We'll discuss how to know when to bid and when to hold back in Chapter Five, but for now, just know that even if someone has been hired for a position, it isn't necessarily over for your chances. It's also possible that the first hire won't work out, in which case, the client will nearly always return to the job ad to review their other prospects before posting a new ad.

Visibility
Step 6 of 8

Who can see your job?

- **Anyone** — Freelancers using Upwork and public search engines can find this job.
- **Only Upwork freelancers** — Only Upwork users can find this job.
- **Invite-only** — Only freelancers you have invited can find this job.

How many freelancers do you need for this job?

- One freelancer
- More than one freelancer

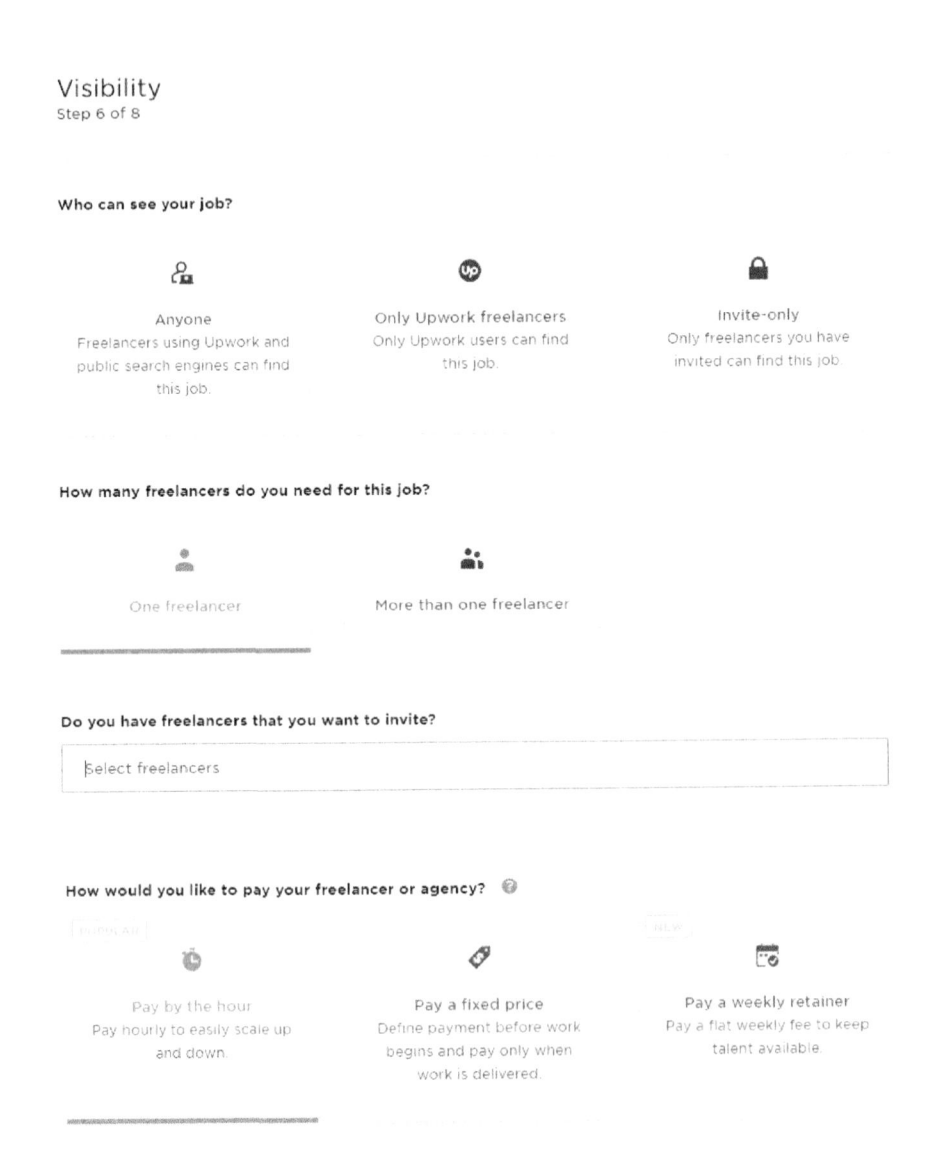

Do you have freelancers that you want to invite?

Select freelancers

How would you like to pay your freelancer or agency?

- **Pay by the hour** — Pay hourly to easily scale up and down.
- **Pay a fixed price** — Define payment before work begins and pay only when work is delivered.
- **Pay a weekly retainer** — Pay a flat weekly fee to keep talent available.

Payment. Now we get to the fun stuff. Here are the basic criteria a client can select:

Hourly, fixed-price, and retainer. Short-term tasks generally tend to be fixed-price, while longer-term or more complex jobs are

often hourly. Fixed-price contracts tend to benefit the client more, while hourly positions are more predictable income for the freelancer. You'll start with the former and hopefully move toward the latter as you build your Upwork portfolio. A retainer is a bit of a hybrid: a client will pay you a fixed weekly fee just to remain available, then any work performed will be billed at an hourly rate.

Level of experience. Look for the jobs that match up with your skill level in that area. Not sure where you land? Start with the beginner jobs: if they seem too elementary, bump up your search level a bit and go for intermediate. Once you feel you can deliver a mastery-level product, go for the expert jobs. This is where you're going to really make your time valuable.

It's *much* better to bid for work that will end up being too easy than for contracts that are just beyond your skill level. You can knock easy tasks out of the park and get phenomenal feedback and client ratings, but if you have to deliver subpar work because you weren't prepared, that negative client feedback will stick with you for a long time. Always calibrate jobs from the bottom up, not the top down.

Timeline. You'll find contracts that are as small as reviewing a product on Amazon or a kid's game in the App Store. On the other side of the spectrum, some clients start hiring for a multiyear freelancing relationship right off the bat. This is an area you'll want to pay attention to and match up with the work-life you wish to have. Is independent contracting something you're doing to pull in a bit of extra cash occasionally, but you don't want it to control you? That's perfectly fine, just stick with projects listed as shorter than a month and less than 30 hours a week. If you want this to become a full-time thing, you might not get picked up for the long-term jobs at first. Build up a solid freelancing resume, and you'll end up turning away more clients than you accept (I turn down about twenty for every one I pick up these days).

Chapter Two Exercise

Log onto Upwork and perform a treasure hunt. I want you to search for the following criteria and then review the ad associated with it. By the time you've worked through each of these, you'll have a much better feel for what's available, how that work is listed, and what clients are willing to pay for it. Getting a feel for Upwork culture is a crucial aspect of long-term success on the platform. If you consistently bid outside of what clients have come to expect as normal, you're not going to win many bids, and the chances of getting frustrated and quitting go up exponentially. That's not what you want. As elementary as this exercise seems, it really will bear fruit if you stick with it.

Remember, all of these should be in the categories of work you're interested in. When you find an ad that fills one of the checkboxes below, "save" the job by clicking on the green heart icon. As you work through more ads, you'll notice new things and want to review what you looked at previously. To revisit any that you've saved, click on the "FIND WORK" option at the top and visit the "Saved Jobs" list.

Treasure Hunt

- 3 fixed-price jobs listed as "entry" level. Record what they pay.
- 3 fixed-price jobs listed as "intermediate" level. Record what they pay.
- 3 fixed-price jobs listed as "expert" level. Record what they pay.
- 3 hourly jobs listed as "entry" level. Record what they pay.
- 3 hourly jobs listed as "intermediate" level. Record what they pay.

Anatomy of an Ad

- ○ 3 hourly jobs listed as "expert" level. Record what they pay.
- ○ 3 jobs based on retainers. See what kind of work in your field is offered on this contract type.
- ○ 3 jobs from a client who has posted two or fewer jobs. List their average feedback rating.
- ○ 3 jobs from a client who has posted 10 jobs or more. List their average feedback rating.
- ○ 3 jobs from a client who has posted 100 jobs or more. List their average feedback rating.
- ○ 3 jobs that are 3 or more days old and have 5 or fewer proposals. These either require highly specific skill sets or have unrealistic client expectations--you'll be able to tell which is which.
- ○ 3 jobs that have been posted in the last 12 hours and have 20 to 50 proposals. It will be nearly impossible to distinguish yourself in these cases, so this is the kind of work you'll want to avoid unless you're first in line.
- ○ 3 jobs from clients with less than a four-star rating. Scroll down to look at the freelancer feedback and see what other contractors are saying about them.

Now that you understand how an ad is created, what each field means, and how it ties into the Upwork search capability from the client side, it's time to shift perspective. In the next chapter, I'll show you how to build your profile to give you the best possible chance of landing this contract.

CHAPTER THREE

Optimizing Your Profile

Upwork has been very intentional about how they've designed their platform. Every piece of information you put down, every filter you include, and every way that you classify yourself impacts how a client can find you, what kinds of jobs you'll see in your feed, and even how competitive you are when bidding. In this section, we'll walk through each aspect of your profile and optimize it to accurately reflect who you are, what your skill sets are, and set you up for success in winning the contracts that are best suited to your talents and experience.

There's an additional potential advantage of a completed profile: the Rising Talent badge. This is a marker Upwork may put on your account if they identify that you have quite a bit of experience in your profession and are just brand new to the Upwork platform. If you're awarded this badge, you'll be bumped up higher in the lists of freelancers Upwork recommends to its clients, and you can bid on jobs that otherwise wouldn't be available to you. There's no guarantee of getting this badge, but the only chance you have is a profile that communicates your expert background.

Making a Good First Impression

Let's start at the top with what I call "first-tier" information. This includes your name, location, title, pay rate, amount earned, job success score (JSS), and qualifications. It also contains the first few lines of your cover letter (which I'll discuss at length in Chapter Five). These are crucial because they're the first things a client sees when reviewing all of the proposals for a job.

Here's an example of how your profile appears to a client browsing all of the proposals she's received:

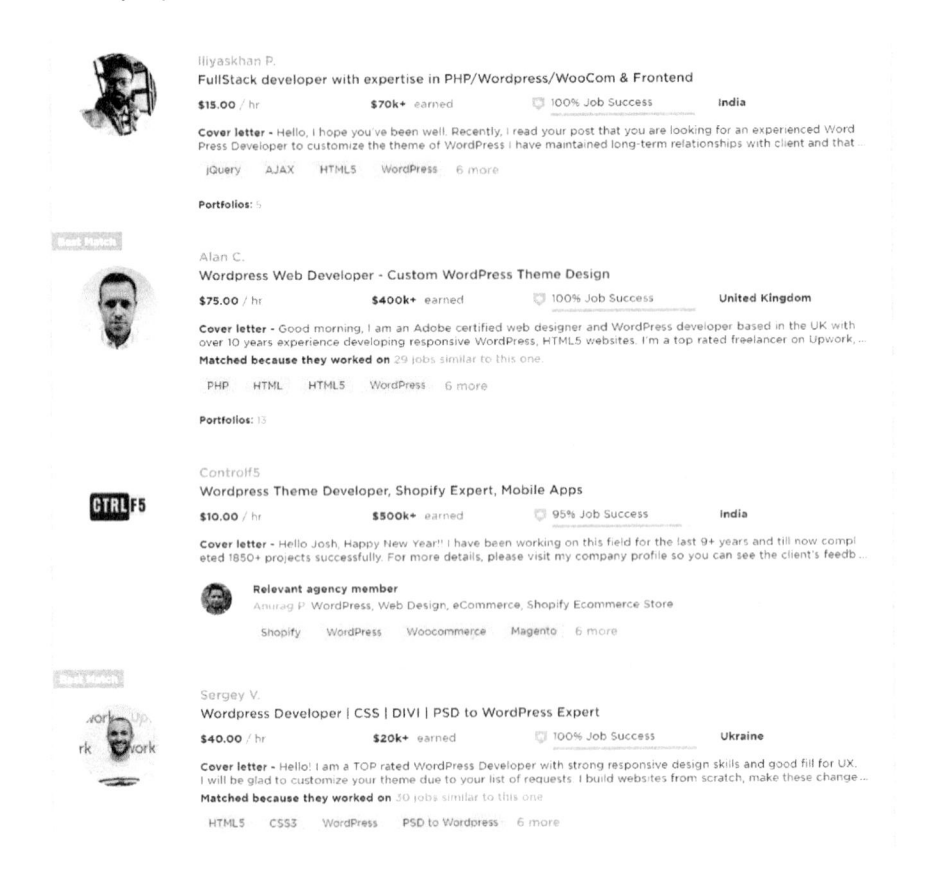

As you can see, these fields are front and center. The majority of freelancers I've coached have not optimized their profile, and this directly (and negatively) impacts their ability to land contracts. In addition to clients, Upwork Job Specialists are also looking for you on their behalf.

Clients can pay Upwork to seek freelancers who are a great fit for their job posting. These specialists can search for information in a variety of ways: closed contract titles and job descriptions, your profile overview, your self-defined skill sets, your portfolio and employment history--you get the idea. You want to make sure that you're giving them all of the information they need to match you to jobs that are well-suited to you.

When clients find and invite you to jobs, you can begin to generate quite a bit of traction. The jobs are coming to you, so you're spending less time searching and more time interviewing. The work has already been filtered to match your skills. Plus, you don't have to pay for any connects to submit a bid if you've been invited to interview, so it's no risk.

How to Structure Your Profile

The little **blue checkmark** beside my name indicates that I've verified my identity. This is critically important, particularly if you're in the United States, because clients can lock down jobs to be seen only by contractors in a specific geographic area. If you live in that area but haven't verified your address, you're out of luck--you won't even see the job, so you don't know what you're missing. Upwork requires address verification via a government-issued ID and a followup video call. This also means that your proper first name will be used, so if you go by your middle name or a nickname, you'll need to clarify that for clients.

Next is your **profile picture**. You should be very selective about which you choose because a poor picture can make you appear distant, cold, uninviting, or unprofessional. Choose an image that's a high-quality close up of your (obviously smiling!) face. Warm tones are preferable to cool tones, and make sure your face is out of the shadows. Paint the picture, from the very first moment, that you're someone they'll enjoy working with. If "pleasant" doesn't describe your photo, change it.

Your **title** is crucial because this is the very first thing (after your name) that clients see when you bid. This might seem simple at first, but it's a bit more complicated.

One of the most fascinating aspects of freelancing is that your work scope can be as broad or as narrow as you like. For example, my last 90 contracts break down like this:

- Article Writing: 27
- Resumes, LinkedIn, and Interview Prep: 13
- Copywriting: 12

- Research: 8
- Ghostwriting: 7
- Test Creation: 6
- Academic Writing: 6
- Editing: 3
- Proofreading: 3
- Unique Tasks: 2
- Project Management: 2
- Social Media Management: 1

Each of these is an entirely different type of work, so how your profile is structured will have a tremendous impact on your ability to land a contract. Upwork now allows you to create up to two specialized profiles (for a total of three), providing more flexibility for various types of work, but we'll get to that in a bit. For the moment, let's focus exclusively on your main profile.

This will be a constantly-evolving iterative process as you explore your interests and develop your niche. When I first began contracting, I focused on what I knew: resumes. I hate writing resumes. I'm good at it, but I don't enjoy the work. I began bidding on jobs that interested me and moved from resume writing to copywriting to article writing, then to research projects, editing and proofreading, ghostwriting books, writing tests, and managing complex projects. If you want to reinvent yourself, this is the place to do it. If you already know your niche and are comfortable there, you don't have to move beyond that.

Think of your profiles as resumes. It's how you represent yourself to potential clients, and it needs to be perfectly targeted to the kind of work you want to do. The only way to get that precise is to work on and update it continually as your career develops.

The overview. This is the area where you get to go all out and talk about yourself! Outline your background, your qualifications, and your skill sets. Mention any specifics, like which coding languages or software systems you're capable of using if you're a techie, or describe your specific style if you're an artist or a writer.

The rest of your profile will tell all the nuts and bolts of your background, but the Overview is where you get to weave a story. I don't mean a literal one, but you can tie together all of the distinct (and often wildly different) talents you bring to the table. Since clients often hire on a per-task basis, the more they get to know you and what you have to offer, the more likely you are to get rehired.

The opening line. "Call me Ishmael." "It was the best of times, it was the worst of times." "In the beginning."

If you want to capture someone's attention and put a bookmark in their mind where your name is, you can't have an average opening line. You should spend as much time on this one sentence as you do for the entire rest of the Overview put together, so 50% of your time is dedicated to figuring out precisely what you want this one sentence to be. Try to distill everything you are and can do down to a single statement. Mine is simple:

"I guarantee satisfaction."

At the end of the day, I'll do whatever it takes to get the client what he or she needs. I've turned off my hourly tracker before and learned a new skill set just so I could take care of something a client needed, even if it was outside the scope of the contract. Don't make a grand promise you won't be able to keep or try to paint yourself as something that you're not. At best case, you'll end up with a string of disappointed clients, subpar feedback, and the inability to successfully operate on the platform.

I also set a very high bar for my work. If a client doesn't like what I've given them, then they don't pay. Period. I've had to eat the cost of a complete project twice during my freelancing career, but the fascinating thing is what happened next. Both clients were so impressed with that policy that they rehired me immediately for subsequent work, which I knocked out of the park.

Upwork values accuracy and puts a high premium on it. Describe who you are, back it up with action, and you'll get five-star feedback. Anyone with a skillset and a good attitude can do well on this platform, but don't try to be something you're not.

The opening paragraph. After your first sentence comes the second (call me Captain Obvious). The rest of your paragraph should expound on that first line: make it short and sweet, but complete the picture. Here's what mine says:

> My primary goal is making sure that you get exactly what you want. Whenever I complete a job, I always ask my clients if I've done everything possible to earn a five-star rating. My favorite response so far has been: "Can I give you six?" That's the kind of quality I provide.

If you spent 50% of your total Overview time on the opening line, you should spend another 25% of it on the rest of the opening paragraph. Remember, every single client and Talent Specialist who sees your profile will read your opening line, and most of them will read a brief introductory paragraph. If you don't capture their attention here, though, they'll never go any further.

Ideal content includes a high-quality piece of feedback from a client (especially if it appears on one of your closed contracts). The bottom line is this: let the client know what you bring to the table.

The body. You also want to include your value proposition here: what is it that you'll do for the client? I tend to be a jack of all trades, and my profile reflects that. If you hire me, you're getting someone skilled in X, Y, and Z, but can take care of pretty much anything else if need be. My career is still evolving: I haven't decided what I want to be when I grow up yet, and I'm ok with that.

If you're a specialist, however, your profile is going to look a bit different. You've found your niche, you're comfortable in it, and you don't plan on going anywhere. There is absolutely nothing wrong with that; you just have a slightly different value proposition. You give the client the strength and rigidity to form building blocks for virtual businesses. You're more likely to be in this area if your occupation requires extensive education (think Master's degree or higher), certification (such as a CompTIA Security+), or experience.

This last criterion is interesting because the types of jobs you'll find on Upwork are virtually unlimited. Quite a few clients will get on Upwork to hire an expert for a quick piece of advice, ask their opinion about something, close out the contract, and go on with their lives. I've worked with HVAC technicians, CNC machinists, delivery truck drivers, bartenders, and construction workers remotely. You can find chefs and welders, plumbers and electricians, servers and housecleaners. If a client needs a specialty, the chances are high that he'll be able to find a freelancer on Upwork with the experience he's looking for.

Arguably the most attractive aspect of Upwork to clients is that they can find *precisely* who they need for only as long as they're needed. They don't have to hire anyone for a more extended period than necessary, aren't limited to the skill sets of their current office staff, and if they don't hire the right person at first, it's easy to try repeatedly at a low cost. Your job is to ensure that you're outlining who you are so the client can evaluate that. If you're not hired, there was a better fit and certainly more work for you out there, so don't get discouraged. If you are hired, you've done your prework and know that it's an excellent fit.

Here's my overview:

> *I guarantee satisfaction.*
>
> *My primary goal is to make sure that you get precisely what you want. Whenever I complete a job, I always ask my clients if I've done everything possible to earn a five-star rating. My favorite response so far has been: "Can I give you six?" That's the kind of quality I provide.*
>
> *I'm an experienced project manager and have hired, evaluated, and overseen hundreds of freelancers on Upwork across dozens of skill sets. If you're looking for someone who is intimately familiar with this platform and can guide your efforts, I can meet your needs.*
>
> *When I taught leadership and communication at Oregon State University as an assistant professor, my students described me as "innovative," "unmatched," "mind-blowingly excellent," and the "best instructor ever." I used to draft and edit the business communications, press releases, and speeches for the current Director of Public Affairs for the US Air Force, General Ed Thomas. If you check out my LinkedIn profile, you'll find a personal endorsement from him where he describes my work as "world-class."*
>
> *My work experience is broad and varied, which gives me a unique perspective from which to pull when creating written content. I've been a professor, an executive assistant, writer, firefighter, proofreader, editor, investigator, military veteran, student, construction worker, retail associate, and*

big-box retail manager, to name a few. I have an extensive background in debate, speech, and blog writing.

I've also worked extensively with resume drafting, editing, and review; the last resume I edited for a client was so successful that he was told by his boss (after he got the job) that she knew she was going to hire him after she first read his resume.

One of my niches is working with high-level admissions and application packages. I've worked with multiple clients at the graduate level and currently have a 100% admissions rate into Harvard, Stanford, Columbia, and INSEAD graduate programs.

One of my greatest strengths lies in critically analyzing complex information, then delivering that content in an easily digestible format specifically tailored to my audience.

I earnestly believe in the power of a good name and reputation; my highest priority is making sure that you, the customer, are satisfied. Please don't hesitate to reach out to me with any questions that you have; I'll be happy to discuss how I can meet your needs or refer you to a more qualified writer if the subject matter calls for it.

Take a moment to review the structure of the writing. In the majority of other applications, you should have one paragraph flow into the next. For your Upwork profile, use a more modular style, where each paragraph can stand on its own and discusses one specific skill set.

Because you're trying to give the Talent Specialists and clients every opportunity to find you, you'll want to write a substantial amount in your Overview. No one is going to read it from top to bottom. It's far more likely that a client will scan through the Overview until she sees something that piques her interest: she'll read that one paragraph, and by the end of those two or three sentences, she should be able to tell whether you're the right fit for the job.

That's what the Overview is supposed to be, but what might be even more important is what it *isn't*, so let's dig in.

The Five Don'ts of Overviews

- **Don't waste your opening line or paragraph.** If this doesn't capture their attention, they won't read the rest.
- **Don't say anything that the client can ascertain by looking at your profile without scrolling.** You might be tempted to highlight if you have the Rising Talent, Top Rated, or other badges, or perhaps quote a lot of client feedback that appears below (a single quote is good, but bulleted lists of reviews aren't). These are fantastic things, but when you mention it on a screen where the client can already see it, you're redundant at best. At worst, you could kill your chances of landing the contract.
- **Don't copy and paste your resume.** You want to tell a story here in a professional, friendly manner.
- **Don't be super technical.** Even if you're a software developer or IT professional, many of the clients looking for you won't be well-versed in what your eight certificates or four programming languages mean. Include these lower in your Overview, but keep the overall tone and content conversational and understandable.

- **Don't try to be flashy.** Some contractors try to make their profile stand out by using exclamation points, words in all caps, or creative punctuation. Avoid this. It isn't professional and doesn't make you stand out any more (at least in a positive way).

Hourly rate. Upwork is an inherently feedback-based platform, meaning one of the tools you have to cultivate is a well-established profile. If you're earning a substantial wage doing the same thing on the outside, you'll likely need to set your rates on Upwork a bit lower until you've received a few solid feedbacks on completed contracts. Once you have an established profile, you can easily charge *more* for your services than you do on the outside, but you've got to put that foundational work in first, and you'll do it much more quickly if you charge lower rates initially.

Always start your rates on the low side until you can justify it with your profile strength. Even if you robust your entire profile and earn a Rising Talent badge, clients might still be reluctant to hire you because they don't know if you're misrepresenting or inflating your job skills. However, when she sees a history of people from her community interacting with your profile and giving you high ratings, you'll be able to raise your rates rapidly to get to what the market will bear.

I wanted to do this full-time, so I pursued it hard. I set my initial rate at $25 an hour and began putting out bids. It took a while to generate those first few clients, but once I got the ball rolling, I kept bidding. I would get a full plate of work, raise my rates by $10 an hour, and immediately begin bidding for jobs that were further out. Because I waited until I had a full plate, I always negotiated pay from a position of strength--I never needed any of the jobs I was bidding on because I was always leaning forward.

The downside of this approach is that it can be easy to overcommit yourself. If you just want to do this on the side, you'll want to try a different approach. Set your rates 10 to 20 percent lower than you think you should be earning until you get those first ten feedbacks. Once that's done, raise your prices to what you think you should be collecting and bid at whatever tempo you feel comfortable with.

Total earnings. The only way to change this is to work your butt off and win, then execute contracts. You're at the right place to make that happen.

Total jobs. This is an excellent indicator of how trusted a freelancer is. Think of it like stars on an Amazon product rating: 4.9 with three reviews isn't bad, but 4.9 at 100 reviews automatically makes you willing to pay a higher premium for that product or service.

If you want to do this full time, you'll likely hit a point where you have all the work you need, and you're not actively searching anymore. Perhaps you're fortunate enough to have one or two contracts that provide forty hours of work per week at your full rate. If that happens, make sure to take a small, fixed-price contract once a month just so you're staying fresh, consistently adding new feedback to your profile, and maintaining your eligibility to earn the Top Rated (or other) badge(s). This also keeps you in a bidding routine; if you ever lose one of those large contracts, you can jump right back into the game and replace it. The longer you go without competing for new work, the longer it will take to shake the rust off and replace it.

Total hours. You can also increase your profile strength and its "trust factor" by working hours. Some freelancers prefer the structure of a fixed-price payment system. There's nothing wrong with that, but don't neglect hourly jobs entirely. This disproportionate balance can create doubt in the client's mind for a brief moment, and sometimes that's all the time you have before they choose someone else. Consider this profile:

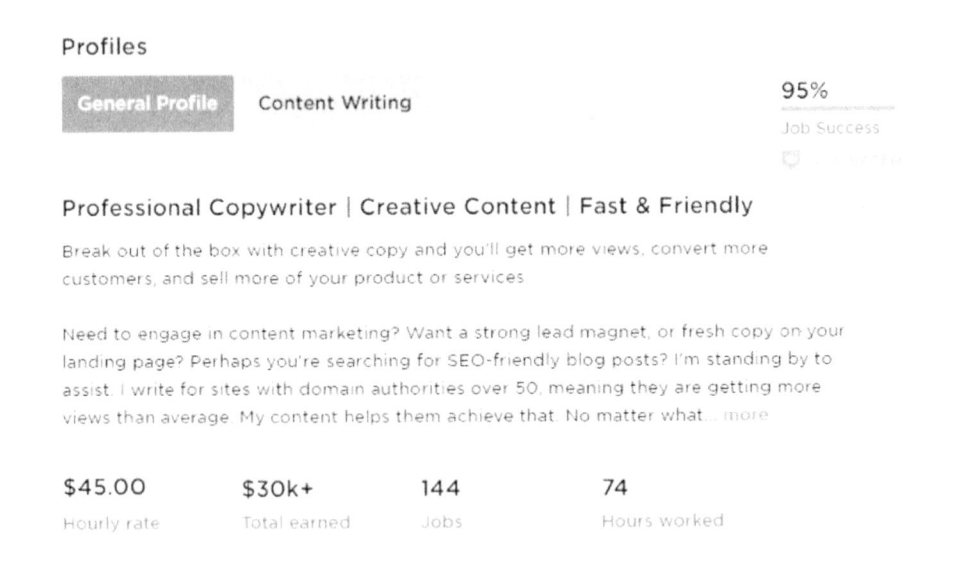

> **Profiles**
>
> **General Profile**   Content Writing   95%
>   Job Success
>
> **Professional Copywriter | Creative Content | Fast & Friendly**
> Break out of the box with creative copy and you'll get more views, convert more customers, and sell more of your product or services
>
> Need to engage in content marketing? Want a strong lead magnet, or fresh copy on your landing page? Perhaps you're searching for SEO-friendly blog posts? I'm standing by to assist. I write for sites with domain authorities over 50, meaning they are getting more views than average. My content helps them achieve that. No matter what... more
>
> $45.00 $30k+   144   74
> Hourly rate   Total earned   Jobs   Hours worked

He's Top Rated with a 95% approval rating--impressive! He's earned $30,000--yes! He's closed 144 jobs--excellent!! He's worked 74 hours--wait, what?

That moment of doubt is what you want to avoid. Develop a well-rounded profile, even if you have to occasionally take lower-paying jobs that will strengthen an aspect of your profile. Remember, this is your career now, and a good name on Upwork is everything if you want to freelance successfully.

Another reason to develop a well-rounded profile is not getting excluded from job opportunities. Clients can select a filter for only freelancers who have logged more than 100 hours. Despite this freelancer being a phenomenal writer, he would be excluded from those search results. The more balanced you are, the more benefits you see.

Privacy settings for profile income display. Upwork defaults to showing how much each contract has been worth: both your rate of pay and the total earned on the contract. This is useful for a few reasons. First, it allows a potential client to see the context of the feedback you've received. Seeing a 5-star rating with a killer comment means a lot more when you can see it's attached to a $2,000 payday than when it could be anything--and there are contracts for $5 on Upwork.

You can toggle this setting to hide it from your profile, but I would only recommend this in rare situations. For example, if you're highly qualified in an area and will be charging a substantial rate (e.g., >$60/hr), but your first few contracts were at a much lower level (e.g., <$20/hr). You don't want to decrease future earnings by setting clients up to expect smaller amounts, so this would be a rare case where hiding your revenues could be the right call. Even in these unique situations, however, you don't want to do this for long--perhaps 3-5 closed contracts in the ballpark you want, then toggle it back on.

As a freelancer, you need to adopt a completely different mindset toward finances than the traditional business world has. In most companies, you're actively discouraged from discussing your rate of pay, it doesn't change often, and the thought of asking for more money from your boss is enough to send many people into an outright panic attack. As a freelancer, you set your rate of pay--and clients expect that. Your rate will change based on the job and the client; Upwork allows you to change any individual contract bid to a quote entirely different than what you indicate on your profile. Getting comfortable with valuing yourself and articulating that is a skill set you *must* develop.

If you feel guilty about asking for a high pay rate, as many do, you can look at things from a client's perspective. Let's say that you earn

$25 an hour at your full-time job and simultaneously advertise your services on Upwork. Your default assumption would be to charge the same rate, but that isn't true. Employers pay onboarding/orientation/training costs, payroll taxes (your employer matches everything that gets deducted from your side of the paycheck), benefits, and finally--your salary. Add all that together, and your employer is actually paying nearly $42 per hour to employ you!

Then, there's what we call the "opportunity cost" of employment. When your company hires you, they're committing to pay you for a certain amount of time or effort (e.g., 40 hours a week for a full-time job). They have committed to spending a certain amount of money, regardless of whether you're gainfully employed or not. In the example above, your $25/hr job requires the employer to set aside $84,000 a year! Employers engage in extensive cost-benefit analyses before they decide to authorize another position simply due to the cost.

Hiring a freelancer skirts the majority of this. Businesses don't have to pay taxes, benefits, or onboarding costs. They don't have to commit to anything beyond paying for an immediate task, so they can flex up and down as business needs arise, making their costs more predictable and ultimately lower. *Instead of committing $84k, they might hire you at $50 an hour* for a month and only spend $8k, making it a win for everyone.

Video introduction. If you are anything other than a media creator (think anything in the videography field), don't worry about making a profile video--it only serves as a liability. If a client needs to conduct a video interview to see how you present yourself or make sure you're well-spoken (some contracts require these traits), they'll request a video interview. If they don't, you're allowing them to do something most of us do: critique the video. People look at your background, your outfit, the lighting on your face. They'll think about the quality of the audio, whether you spoke too much or too little, or whether they liked the way your voice sounded. It's possible that this could do you some good, but (other than media creators), there isn't much you could showcase here that would further convince someone you'd do a good job.

However, if you are a media person, this can be the perfect place to showcase some of your best work. You likely already have a video, or can produce one relatively easily. If you decide to do this, keep in mind that you want it to be short, sweet, and to the point. You should cleanly showcase a broad range of your skills, but you shouldn't try to cram everything here. Give them the best taste you can, then get out. Even if they're hiring you to produce a documentary, they don't want to watch one.

Availability. You can choose two primary settings: Available and Unavailable. If it's the former, you can indicate one of three levels: more than 30 hrs/week, less than 30 hrs/week, and as needed - open to offers. If it's the latter, you can indicate the date you estimate you'll become available again.

Upwork uses this to filter how they promote your profile to clients who are sending invites for jobs. If you mark yourself as unavailable, you'll be dropped from the recommendation list. If you're available, you'll appear in the listings; the more open you are, the fewer restrictions there will be in what kind of jobs for which you're eligible.

Languages. This is a crucial aspect of your profile and a primary determiner in the kinds of jobs you'll get. The majority of you will likely be Native or Bilingual in English, but if you list any other languages, be sure that you can back up whatever level you list. Remember, it's <u>always</u>

better to knock something out of the park and exceed expectations than fall just a bit short. There are four levels of proficiency for language:

- **Basic** - I write in this language decently.
- **Conversational** - I write and speak this language well.
- **Fluent** - I write and speak this language almost perfectly.
- **Native or Bilingual** - I write and speak this language perfectly, including colloquialisms.

Education. Education matters. If you can imagine a particular job task out there, you'll eventually find a contract on Upwork for it. If someone wants to evaluate the educational quality of a specific major at a particular institution of higher learning during a unique set of years, just having that listed could make you a shoo-in for an easy job (yes, I've seen contracts like this out there). If you didn't attend college but graduated high school, consider putting that there. Even if you just have a GED, this can be a feather in your cap.

Remember, we're not worried about checkboxes for the sake of checkboxes. We want to give the client everything they need to hire you for the broadest range of potential jobs. When you consider the full range of individual tasks posted by all of the businesses and clients on Upwork, it's easy to see how any additional hiring factor could make the difference in getting you a contract.

Groups. Upwork used to have several groups that provided a community of prescreened freelancers for clients to browse. All but one of these has been eliminated; the only one left is the US Military Veterans group. If you're eligible, sign up, and they'll vet you (pun intended). This can be valuable; I've been hired off this group for two contracts that required military experience. If you're not a vet, though, don't worry about this.

Talent clouds. I mentioned an employer's onboarding costs earlier. Large enterprise Upwork clients often find that working with clients who have experience with their company can consistently yield better, more efficient results. There's less spinup with each contract, and freelancers can often be paired with the same project manager.

Being accepted into a talent cloud is a big deal because it increases your chance of subsequent contracts, and repeat business is always good. You'll also be at the top of the list for invitations from

About the client

Upwork Enterprise Client

Payment method verified

Indeed

★★★★★
4.97 of 5891 reviews

United States
Stamford 08:43 am

2779 jobs posted
93% hire rate, 5 open jobs

$10M+ total spent
9,982 hires, 404 active

$10.04/hr avg hourly rate paid
474,929 hours

Member since Feb 22, 2017

that client, meaning you don't have to pay for connects. Finally, you can get email notifications of new job postings from the enterprise employer, even if they haven't explicitly invited you.

The only way to become part of a talent cloud is to complete a contract with the business that owns the cloud. If you see a job posting from an enterprise client, an excellent strategy is to lower your bid slightly to increase your chances of being hired for that first contract. Knock it out of the park, and you're in.

Here's an example of what an Enterprise client's "About" section would look like on a job post.

Work history & feedback. This is the single most crucial aspect of your Upwork experience, hands down. You have some control over it (we'll discuss that later when I walk you through a full contract), but for the most part, what happens here is exclusively determined by your clients. The good news is that your clients are going to base their feedback on how well you worked out, so this is ultimately in your hands as well.

There are several pitfalls to avoid here. Some clients post jobs for simple tasks: leaving an Amazon product review, or rating a mobile app in the App Store. They offer low pay ($5 - $10 for the total job) and a 5-star review. This can be tempting when you're starting and trying to land your first few contracts, but I recommend avoiding these jobs. The most critical reason is that the title of the contract often very clearly advertises that this is a virtually worthless contract that is blatantly gaming the system--and that goes on your profile permanently. You'll gain a temporary bump in ratings, but the tradeoff of compromising your work history quality is rarely worth it.

If you've gotten yourself in a bind and have a low Job Success Score, you might have to rebuild from scratch--and this is a time where considering contracts like this could be an option. If you've dropped below an 80% approval rating, you're most likely not going to be considered for contracts related to your primary field. Because Upwork ties your profile to your identity (as they should), you can't just start over--you must overcome it. Other than this limited set of circumstances, however, avoid these. We'll talk more about a full contract life cycle in Chapter Six, particularly regarding how to close a contract successfully.

Portfolio. A robust portfolio is one of the hallmarks of a complete profile, but the benefits can be a bit indirect. This area is crucial for visual fields such as graphic designers, photographers, and videographers. More traditional fields will struggle--it's challenging to impress someone with your portfolio of accounting clerk tasks, for example.

I always recommend that you put at least four projects in your profile because that maximizes the amount of space available to you. Having a robust portfolio communicates you're serious about being a freelancer and experienced in your field--even if you never have a single client click on any of the items you've placed there.

Think of it this way: if someone rolled up to a first date and they were missing the rear passenger door on their car, would you have a positive or negative opinion of them? Most likely pretty negative, even though you could date that person for a year and never actually use that door. Just because it doesn't directly contribute to you being hired for an individual contract doesn't mean that it doesn't provide an "entourage effect" that increases your long-term chances of success.

Each portfolio entry doesn't have to be very robust, so don't be intimidated. Even if you work in a field that isn't as easy to display as photography or graphic design, think about projects you've worked on or individual tasks that you've mastered. Virtually anything can go in this place, so mentally go through your work experience, what you want to be hired for, and find the four best matches.

Skills. The skills section is both critical and dynamic. Critical, because this is one of the most crucial cornerstones for how clients and Talent Specialists match you to jobs. The #1 most important rule for this section is always to have it fully populated with ten skill sets. Upwork utilizes predictive text when you're filling out this section, so if you've exhausted your occupational vocabulary and still have fewer than ten, simply go down the alphabet. Enter an "A," then see what pops up. Scroll down the list, then repeat with B, and so forth. I guarantee you'll be able to find ten skills.

This section is also dynamic, and you should check it every month to ensure it's still current. Sometimes your job focus changes; this ability to quickly evolve is one of the most significant advantages of contracting. At times you'll discover terms that more appropriately describe you; update them accordingly. The bottom line is that you should never let this go out of date.

Before I go into the next section, I need to identify another core area where your expectations should change as you transition from traditional employment to freelancing.

Corporate America has fallen in love with box-checking, but in developing a quantifiable, apples-to-apples comparison system, it can be easy to forget that not all apples are of equal quality. Someone who did the bare minimum to check all of the boxes isn't even the same league as someone who worked his ass off to develop a stellar set of skills.

Freelancing, in general, operates off of merit-based employment rather than a checkbox-based approach. If you can do the job, clients rarely care what kind of educational pedigree you have. Someone who has a Masters in Computer Science but can't solve your IT problems simply won't compete with a high school dropout who has spent the last ten years teaching himself the ins and outs of IT. As a client, all I care about is whether the person I hire can knock it out of the park, and the most important measuring stick for me is client feedback.

Understanding this perspective shift is crucial as you move into the next section, where we discuss checkboxes. Using checkboxes to communicate merit is a far different animal from using checkboxes for their own sake. As you develop your profile, remember that your main goal in this section is to communicate competence with every word.

Pre-packaged projects. If you have a set of skills that's more modular, listing a pre-packaged project can be an excellent strategic move. Let's say you transcribe text from audio recordings and charge a certain amount per hour, or you're an animator and know it typically costs $X to create a thirty-second video. This can serve as a type of "pre-interview," where a client searching for the right freelancer can see your work and get an approximate quote without you having to do a thing.

The less modular your skills are, the less useful this section is, and that's not a problem. Remember, if it isn't useful to you, it probably isn't helpful to anyone you'd be competing against.

Testimonials. This allows you to bring in client testimonials from non-Upwork sources. It's very beneficial in a few specific circumstances:

- If you've never been a freelancer, but have coworkers, customers, or clients who would endorse you (for example, like you'd see on LinkedIn).
- If you're a freelancer who is coming from another platform.

To populate this section, click on the plus icon adjacent to it. Upwork will provide a form with fields for the client's first and last name, title, business email address, LinkedIn profile, the type of project you completed for them, and space where you can write a message to your client. It's always best to reach out to a client before sending them a form email and making sure that they're willing to give you a positive endorsement. If the client expresses any privacy concerns, reassure them that their last name won't appear on the feedback, and their

LinkedIn profile is only for Upwork team validation purposes (they don't want you endorsing yourself via email) and won't be linked to them.

Certifications. Certifications for the sake of certifications mean nothing (even though that award-winning pie I baked in the 2nd grade was indeed a true work of art). In certain industries, however, these are the gold standard of quality. Network Security is arguably the biggest purveyor of educational certificates, and the majority of these have real value. If you have CISSP, CompTIA Security+, or CISM, for example, you'll likely never lack for work.

You're the best judge of whether a certificate has value in your industry or not. If it does, by all means--add it. If it doesn't, less is more here. This is the one area I recommend leaving blank if you don't have something that will add demonstrable value to it.

Employment history. This is the closest you'll see to a traditional resume on someone's Upwork profile, but it should be written differently. In a conventional resume, you want to pack every inch of white space with bullets that are very condensed, sometimes to the point of being nearly unreadable to people outside of that industry.

Exchange bullets for narratives here: simply tell a client what they should know about your professional background in one or two paragraphs. Write in the first person (e.g., "I did X") rather than the third person (e.g., "Johnny did X"). Be sophisticated enough that it's professionally written, but don't be too conversational--avoid slang. Explain abbreviations the first time you use them, like this: "Did you know that NASCAR (Non-Athletic Sport Centered Around Rednecks) doesn't actually stand for that?"

The goal of this section is to make reading it as easily digestible as possible for the client. Remember that the *moment* a client gets frustrated, overwhelmed, or confused, they're going to skip the entire section. That kills the value of what you have there, so you have to put in some effort here. The good news is that past entries in this section don't change unless you choose to update or rewrite it. Put in a solid effort upfront, drop it in your profile, and then forget about it--you shouldn't have to do anything here if you wrote it correctly the first time.

Other experiences. This is a bit of a catch-all for anything that didn't easily fit into other categories. For example, if you have a military tech school that didn't result in a certification or diploma, include it here. If you went through an intense week-long training session to better yourself in a particular area, this is the perfect place for that. Conferences, conventions, teaching opportunities--all of those can be listed here.

Specialized profiles. Specialized profiles have all the same features as your main profile. Their primary benefit lies in allowing a contractor to present themselves as specialists in various areas, and you can even set different pay rates. You can also select which contracts appear on your specialized profiles. I have two: in addition to my writing/project management main profile, I have one as a professional researcher and a third that focuses explicitly on ghostwriting. If you work in a variety of independent niches, you should consider creating a specialized profile for each one. This gears you more specifically to particular types of work, and the better a match you can make yourself for a specific contract, the better your chances of getting it.

That being said, most freelancers (especially those starting out), should *not* create secondary profiles. Remember that Upwork is an inherently feedback-based platform, and specialized profiles feature only the work and experiences applicable to them. It's much better to create a single, robust profile and immediately begin bidding than spend hours or days creating subsequent profiles before you're steadily landing contracts.

Your Job Success Score (JSS). This is arguably the most critical metric in your Upwork career. Upwork's Job Success Score, or JSS, is the percentage score shown near the top of your profile. It is the single most important element when it comes to landing contracts on Upwork. In this chapter, I'll explain what it is, how it's calculated, what you can do to maximize your JSS, and how to avoid and recover from common pitfalls.

There are a lot of details in this section, and it can get complicated quickly. Don't be overwhelmed. In fact, if you're just starting out, you should only read until the "If You Encounter Problems" section. Don't go further. Everything up to that point will give you the tools you need to succeed. However, if you encounter problems (boy, this is convenient), go to that section and start reading.

Joshua B.
Springfield, OR

View profile

Ghostwriting

Online Research

All work

99%
Job Success

TOP RATED PLUS

The exact algorithm isn't something Upwork reveals; they want to keep people from gaming the system. If you're in the Upwork world for long enough, you're going to hear lots of complaining about the JSS, but it's generally undeserved. I've found that complaints always come from one of three groups of people:

- Freelancers who are generally crappy and the JSS is designed to penalize.
- Freelancers who don't understand how it's calculated or used and misinterpret what's going on.
- Freelancers who have hit common pitfalls and don't know how to recover.

I can't help you with the first one, but I can with the other two.

How the JSS is Calculated

You're not going to get a JSS until you've typically completed between five and eight contracts. Sometimes it takes longer than this, but that's the norm. This window is critical, and I'll explain why in a minute.

The basic calculation looks like this:

$$(successful\ contract\ outcomes - negative\ contract\ outcomes) / total\ outcomes$$

Let's say you've closed eight contracts. Seven of them went well, but one went completely sideways. The approximate score would look like this:

$$(7 - 1) / 8 = 75\%$$

As you can see, negative contracts have a disproportionate effect on your JSS. Upwork designs it this way because they want to strongly encourage satisfaction, and bad outcomes are penalized.

Your JSS is calculated according to three different timelines: 6-, 12-, and 24-month histories. Unless you've been freelancing for less than six months, these will usually produce different values, and Upwork takes the highest value. These calculations are run every two weeks.

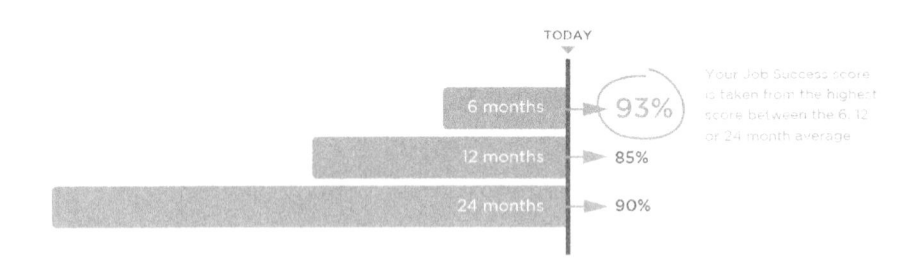

```
                          TODAY
                            ▼
                                        Your Job Success score
        6 months    →  93%              is taken from the highest
                                        score between the 6, 12
        12 months   →  85%              or 24 month average.

        24 months   →  90%
```

Knowing this timeline will be crucial when I discuss strategies for recovering from a poor JSS.

How Contracts are Weighted

There is, of course, quite a bit of latitude in how this is calculated. Perhaps your negative contract outcome wasn't a 1-star rating; maybe it was 3.5 stars, and Upwork won't penalize you as much for that. Always strive to earn the best rating you can; even if that isn't five stars, four is still considered a positive outcome.

The contract value is also considered. Let's say a client hired you for a $75 job, and the poop hit the oscillator: you got one star and a nasty comment. That will be given far less weight than a $10,000 contract that's been going on for a year. If you get negative feedback after a $75 job, it could be due to a number of reasons, but if you get dinged after earning $10k, you must have done something pretty bad.

Long-term clients can provide a boost to your score. If you go to Find Work > My Stats, you'll find a statistic indicating the percentage of your clients who are long-term. When you're just starting out, it'll be 0%, and it'll probably hang out there for a while. That's not a problem: some freelancers prefer short-term projects and structure long-term careers out of those. Having no long-term contracts doesn't penalize you, but if you've got them, it can provide a boost.

One of the things I appreciate about Upwork is that they want to cull bad clients and take an active role in making sure that happens. When a contract is closed, you get to rate the client as well, and clients with a history of negative feedback and poor collaboration can be flagged or even removed from the platform. If either of those happens, that client's feedback won't count against your JSS.

Avoiding JSS Pitfalls

Upwork is a feedback-intensive platform. Get good ratings and you'll thrive. If you don't, however, you can knock yourself out of an Upwork freelancing career pretty quickly. If you follow these best practices, you'll avoid the most common JSS pitfalls that get new freelancers into trouble.

Focus on establishing your JSS. When you first begin, you can assume you've got 5 to 8 contracts before you get a JSS, and this is the time to invest in it. You should track these jobs closely and make giving your client a great experience a priority above literally everything else.

The amount of money you're being paid is irrelevant. The type of work you're doing is largely irrelevant. Landing and executing entry-level contracts when you've billed yourself as an expert doesn't matter. The only thing that matters right now is getting good feedback.

Choose the right contracts. There are two sides to this coin: picking the right clients and picking the right tasks. What you should look for in a client is covered in Chapter Four. The jobs you look for should be short-term, fixed-price, and consist of things you know you can knock out of the park. Underbidding, under-promising, and overdelivering at this point are important. At this stage of the game, you're not trying to maximize profitability--you're setting yourself up to maximize profitability for the rest of your Upwork career, which could last for years.

Let the client end the contract. Any contract can be terminated by either the freelancer or the client. However, only the party that initiates the conclusion is required to give feedback; it's optional for the other party. If you end the contract, there's no pressure for the client to rate you, even if she feels positively toward you. However, if you let her end the contract, she'll be required to enter values in all of those fields. (The flip side of this is that if you think a contract is going to go badly, you've tried everything to fix it and nothing is working, you should end the contract—that decreases your chance of the client leaving negative feedback.)

If a client doesn't leave feedback, you face two problems. The first is the loss of a potential positive--you've earned a rating, but you're not receiving it. The second is introducing a possible negative: although Upwork doesn't penalize you for one or two contracts that end without feedback, if it becomes a trend, your JSS will drop.

When you've sent the client the final deliverable, ask the client the five-star question I introduced in Chapter Four:

> *"At the end of a contract, I always like to ask whether I've done everything possible to earn five stars. If I haven't, would you let me know before we close out? Your satisfaction is my top priority, and I'd like to fix anything that I can."*

This implies that everything is done from your end, and they can end the contract whenever they like. I tend to get a pretty high rate of client-initiated contract terminations with this approach, which triggers client feedback and boosts your JSS. Occasionally, I'll have a client come back with a positive response ("No, you were great! I really enjoyed working with you!") but then do nothing. The contract just sits.

Keep in mind that there's no rush. You've obviously knocked this contract out of the park, and Upwork won't penalize you for leaving a contract open with no activity for a few weeks or even a couple of months. Once a week has gone by, you can ping the client. Politely explain how vital feedback is to your Upwork career, and it helps your profile out if the client closes everything out and marks "Contract successfully completed" as the reason for it ending. I usually say something like this:

> Hi! If there's nothing else I can do for you on this contract, would you mind closing it out?
>
> It looks better in Upwork's eyes if the client closes the contract out and marks that the job was successfully completed, and the feedback I get really helps me as a freelancer.

If you've done a good job for a client, you'll find that they're usually very willing to help you out, especially if it doesn't cost them anything. Don't hesitate to tell them that good feedback will help you and is much appreciated--just don't come across as demanding, pressuring, or begging.

If the client disappears, I'll typically wait two more weeks, then ping them again and wait a week for a response. At this point, it's been a month since the last contact, and if they haven't respond by now, they're not going to. I'll proactively close the contract from my side at that point and move on.

If You Encounter Problems

Ideally, your first eight contracts will go flawlessly, and you'll have eight five-star reviews with glowing comments. If you do everything I've told you so far, you'll maximize your chances of that happening. That's not always the case, though.

You always want to maintain at least a 90% JSS. This puts you on track for the Top Rated badge, keeps you from being eliminated from client search filters, and makes you attractive to clients when submitting bids. If you drop below this, you've put yourself in a hole that's going to be difficult to dig your way out of.

Let's revisit how the JSS is (approximately) calculated and the earlier example.

$$(successful\ contract\ outcomes - negative\ contract\ outcomes) / total\ outcomes$$

If you've closed eight contracts and seven of them went well, but one went badly, your approximate score would look like this:

$$(7 - 1) / 8 = 75\%$$

To get back to a 90% JSS, you're going to have to close out a total of 20 contracts, 19 of which need to be good.

$$(19 - 1) / 20 = 90\%$$

Earlier, I mentioned the importance of watching these first eight contracts like a hawk. If one of them goes badly, you need to react quickly. The good news is you likely have a bit of time before your JSS publishes, and at this point, having no JSS is better than a low

JSS. Go to the search feature of your job feed, click in the search bar, and hit "Enter."

You'll see am extensive listing of every job posted on Upwork for which you're eligible. In this case, I've got nearly 27,000.

Click on the "Filters" button and you'll see a screen that looks like this:

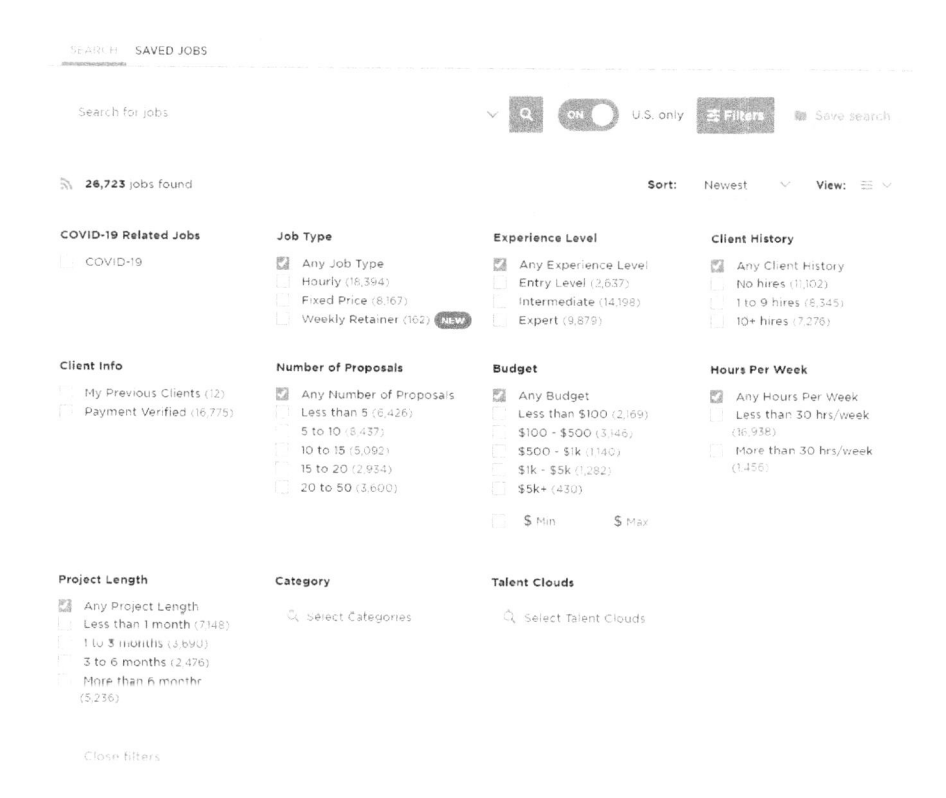

Click the "Fixed Price" option under Job Type, then go to the Budget column and enter a maximum amount of $5. Close the filters, and you'll see this:

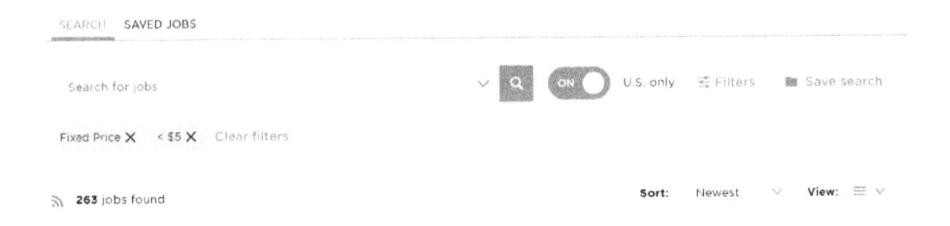

With those two filters applied, I've eliminated 99 percent of the jobs. Your goal is to find 12 more jobs that are easy to win, easy to execute, and the client has a history of offering feedback to freelancers. Here are a few jobs that fit the bill:

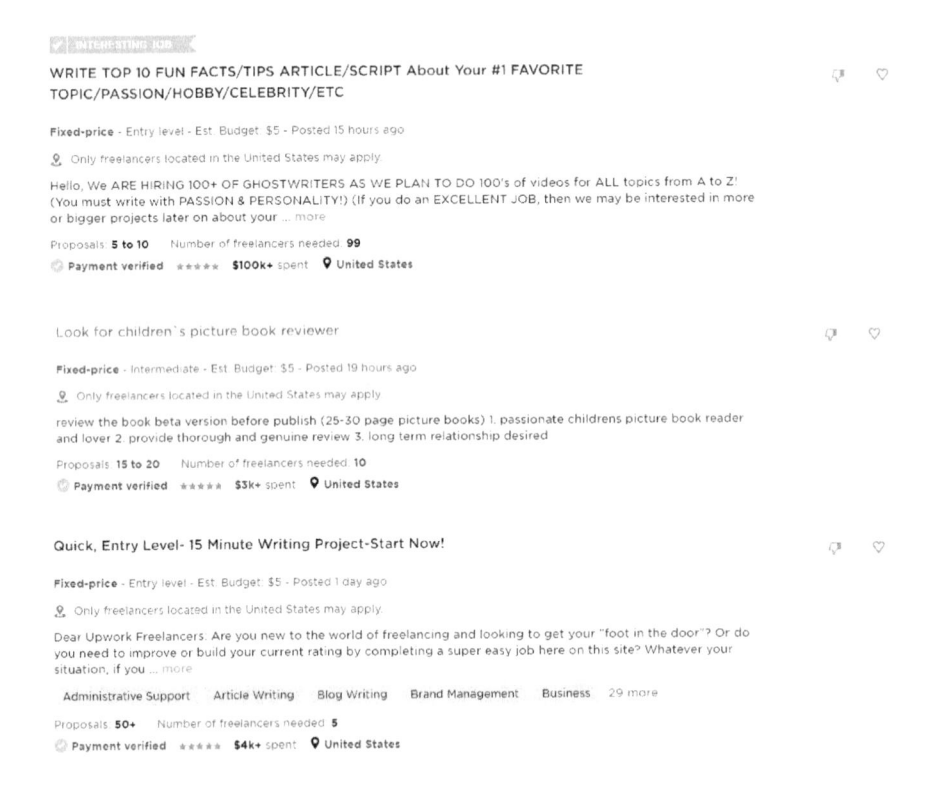

None of these jobs would take more than a few minutes to apply for, win, and complete. You might not be able to find 12 active ones right off, so save your search (there's a button next to the Filters button at the top) and check it a couple of times a day until you've knocked these out. Of course, you can continue to bid on normal projects in the meantime, but the priority is getting 12 more contracts procured before your JSS is published.

If you do that, your JSS can publish and show 75%, but that's fine. You've landed all the contracts you need to bump it up to 90%. Complete them, knock them out of the park, get five-star ratings, and when the JSS recalculates in two weeks, you should be at 90% and back in business.

Recovering from a Poor JSS

Caveat: This section is complicated, detailed, and can be both frustrating and discouraging. If you find yourself throwing your hands in the air, skip to the last paragraph, right before the section titled "The Crucial Role of Timing."

Some freelancers find themselves with a poor JSS and quite a few contracts under their belts. Fixing this requires a similar approach to what I've outlined above, but with one significant twist: you need to own your poor JSS to the clients that made it happen.

Negative feedback is only as permanent as the client wants to make it. Upwork has an option where you can reopen feedback on a closed contract so the client can go back in and change it. With this in mind, your first step is to review the contracts where you didn't receive feedback at all. Reach out to them and see if they'd be willing to go in and rate your performance. You could be getting penalized for having too many contracts without any feedback at all, and this is relatively easy to fix. You don't have to get feedback on each one. Upwork states that it only begins to count contracts without feedback if they become excessive; if that's the case with you, you might only need a couple to change before you get dropped back into the "non-excessive" safety zone.

If you've done that and aren't getting the results you need, you'll have to something that's going to take a lot of humility. Revisit the contracts that went bad. Go back to those clients, own what went wrong on your part, and apologize for your role in it. Don't start a fight, don't blame them, and don't even bring up what they did wrong. I don't care if they were 90 percent wrong and you only had 10 percent of the fault. Keep the focus on you and own your 10 percent. Tell them what you've learned and will do differently in the future.

Once you have a dialogue going and it seems to be going well, ask them if they would be willing either to give you a second chance with a small task or change their feedback. Don't beg, but there's no harm in being clear about how much your JSS is negatively impacting you, and it's caused you to realize you need to change a few things.

You won't get replies from all of the clients, and you won't get positive responses from everyone who does write back. However, reversing even a single negative feedback can have a tremendously positive effect. Here are two examples:

Example 1: 70% JSS with 20 closed contracts, 3 negative.

$$(17 - 3) / 20 = 70\%$$

Now, the same situation with one contract you've turned around:

$$(18 - 2) / 20 = 80\%$$

You just gave yourself a 10 percent boost by adopting that approach.

Example 2: 73% JSS with 30 closed contracts, 4 negative.

$$(26 - 4) / 30 = 73\%$$

Now, the same situation with one contract you've turned around:

$$(27 - 3) / 30 = 80\%$$

Once again, a single reversal can have a substantial impact. This isn't an easy thing: humbling yourself in front of someone you disagreed with isn't something anyone enjoys. However, let's look at both of those examples again and see how hard it would be to work your way back to the same level by executing new contracts.

Example 1: 70% JSS with 20 closed contracts, 3 negative.

$$(27 - 3) / 30 = 80\%$$

In this case, you'd have to close out an additional ten contracts to replace what you could gain with one reversal. If you want to get to 90%, you're going to have to close out 60 contracts, the next 40 of which need to be positive.

Example 2: 73% JSS with 30 closed contracts, 4 negative.

$$(36 - 4) / 40 = 80\%$$

In this case, you'd also have to close out another ten contracts to get to 80%. You'd have to get to 80 closed contracts, 76 of which were positive, to get to 90%.

The reason I present all of this is not to be discouraging. It's not even to encourage you to engage in some Herculean effort to close out fifty contracts in a month. I want you to see how heavily negative feedback can impact you. Understanding the weight of what you're dealing with will help you bid more carefully and be far more willing to work with a client to reach a positive resolution than just give up and take the negative feedback. From this point on, the news about recovering from a poor JSS gets much more encouraging.

The Crucial Role of Timing

If you're normal, the previous section was probably pretty discouraging. It can be very difficult to dig yourself out of a JSS hole. However, remember that you don't have one JSS--you have three. One is based on all of the contracts you've closed in the last 6 months and ignores the rest, one is based on all of your contracts in the past 12 months and ignores anything older than that, and the final one is based on your 24-month contract history.

Find the date that your most recent negative feedback was received. Six months after that, one of your job success scores won't count it. If you close out even one contract between here and there and get a good review, your six-month JSS could be 100%.

Upwork is all about giving you a second chance, and the timing of the JSS windows is the most significant evidence of that. The bad news is that this takes time. Six months can be quite a long time to wait, but you might not have to go that long. If you want to find out when your JSS will go positive, map out all of your contracts on a spreadsheet. Put the titles of the contracts in the first column. In the second, identify if it was good or bad. In the third, put the date that it closed out.

Start with the oldest negative score, then count *forward* from there (i.e., all of the ones closed out since). Run the JSS equation with those numbers. Whatever is there is the worst JSS you'll have, assuming you don't get any more negative reviews, and it only goes up from here. Now, move to the first positive feedback after that one.

Rerun the JSS equation. That's the JSS you'll have the day after that oldest negative review drops off.

Repeat that process with each negative feedback: calculate from that review until now, first including it, then starting from the first contract after that one closed out. Once you've done this, you'll have a roadmap of when your six-month JSS values will change, assuming no new contracts.

Here's the bottom line: you can recover from a poor JSS, and your six-month JSS window is your best shot at doing that. However, you've got to give your all during this time and earn those positive reviews. You can turn your JSS around at any time, as long as you're willing to work and wait those six months for it.

How to Explain a Poor JSS

Although it will take half a year to reset the six-month JSS, you can continue to bid during this time. However, if you've got a sub-80% JSS, any client with a legitimate job who considers hiring you will likely ask why your success score is so low. You need to answer that professionally, completely, but most importantly--truthfully. Own your responsibility in it: don't give excuses. I'll give you a few examples below to help frame possible reasons, but *only use those that truthfully apply to your situation.*

- If you have few or no negative reviews, but a lot of closed contracts without feedback at all, you can point to that. Say, *"I didn't realize how important getting feedback was, and I closed multiple contracts in a row without asking the clients for feedback."*
- If you have negative reviews, own what went wrong. Say, *"I had a contract go badly. I made X mistake and didn't handle Y well.*

I learned Z, and that's how I'm going to handle that situation differently in the future."

Don't justify yourself in either of these situations. Do not badmouth the client. At this point, the client you're talking to identifies more strongly with the client you had an issue with than he is with you. If you whine about how terrible the other client was, this one isn't going to give you a shot. It's obvious you haven't learned your lesson, and he's not going to hire you and watch things go badly for him as well.

As a client, I'd consider hiring a freelancer who had a poor JSS as long as they could tell me why it had happened, what they had learned, and what they would do differently. The best antidotes to a poor JSS are good performance, time, and humility.

The Benefits of a Good JSS

The most significant benefit of having a good JSS is earning the Top Rated or higher badges. These are calculated based on a rolling 16-week window; as long as you have a 90% or higher JSS in 13 of those 16 weeks and no account holds, you'll earn the Top Rated badge. It might take a couple of extra weeks to populate after you've earned it, but be patient and it'll come through eventually.

This badge comes with several crucial benefits. Unlike the experience you had as an ignored, neglected newcomer, Upwork suddenly values you. You get access to live chat and customer support, you can have issues resolved more quickly, and you get a tremendous boost in credibility when it comes to any disputes.

Arguably the most notable feature of the Top Rated badge is the ability to selectively remove reviews from your profile. You can eliminate one negative piece of feedback from your profile every ten weeks, as long as you've closed out ten or more contracts between removals. You can choose to remove the review from public view and your JSS or from public view only. Generally speaking, you'll always want to remove it from your JSS. However, you might run across a situation where a client left a five-star review, but their comment was unprofessional or embarrassing in some way. Upwork will allow you to remove the comment but continue to count the contract rating toward your JSS.

Upwork has been putting a lot of emphasis on helping clients search for and invite freelancers to interview for their jobs. You want to be in the position to receive invitations, which means optimizing your profile and removing every barrier to being invited. Clients can filter freelancers based on JSS, and the most restrictive filter limits the contractors they see to those with 90% or higher JSS. If you've got 90%, you're in this club.

Improving from 90% to 100% generally helps your competitiveness on individual contracts, particularly when you begin increasing what you charge. You want to be able to justify asking for premium rates, and a 99% JSS can be worth $30 an hour more than a 91% JSS, depending on the contract. Always push to keep your JSS high and maintain it.

Keeping Your JSS Stable

At the end of the day, the JSS is a tool to measure how well freelancers are meeting their clients' needs. No tool will ever be perfect, but as evaluations go, the JSS is pretty solid. It measures the right metrics in the right ways and is a pretty fair way to compare freelancers across the board. My goal in teaching this lesson isn't to teach you how to game the system. I only want you to know how to use it effectively, as you should with any tool.

The bottom line is simple: if you keep your clients happy, you'll have a good JSS. Managing client relationships is crucial to success, and we'll discuss strategies for that in the next chapter.

Secrets of an Upwork Master

Chapter Three Exercise

One of the best ways to create your profile is to look at what winners are already doing. Visit www.Upwork.com/l/us (that's an "L" but won't work capitalized). You'll see a page that looks like this:

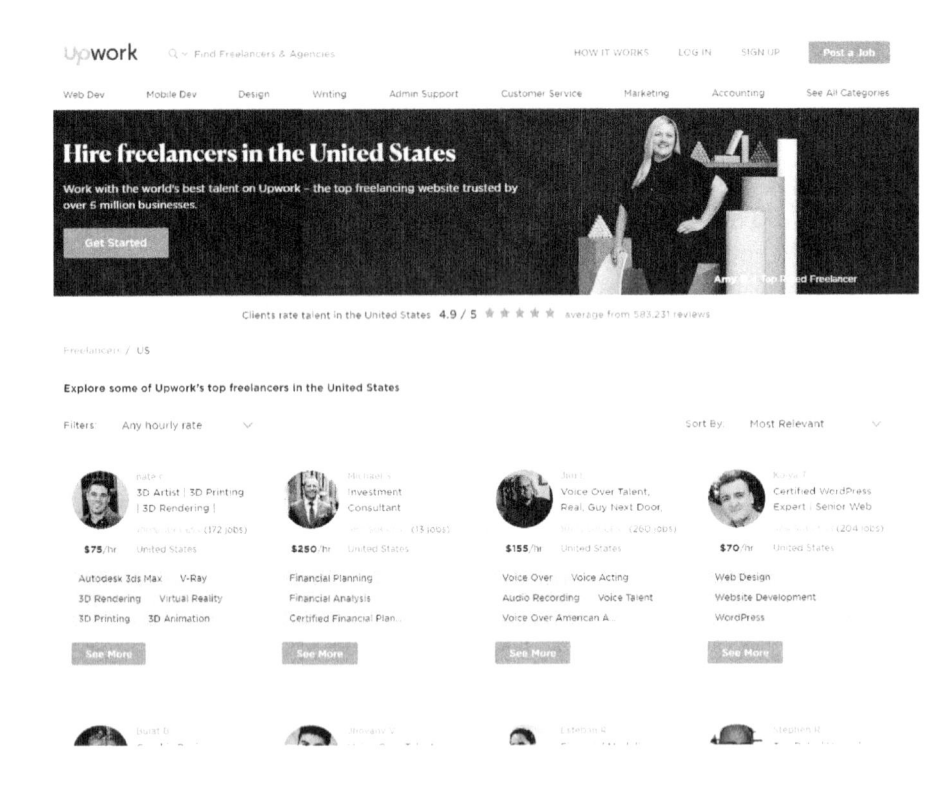

Use the top banner categories to find the type of work you're interested in, then check out the top five freelancers in your area. Find what seems compelling to you and copy those aspects of their profiles as you design your own.

CHAPTER FOUR

Finding the Right Contract

Congratulations! Making it to this point means you have nearly every tool you need to become a successful freelancer! Whether you want to make this a full-time career change or are just looking for a side hustle for additional cash, you've got a robust toolbox in hand and are ready to take on the world.

Most of what you need now is gaining skill in using those tools, and that's what we'll delve into here. The few remaining tools you require will also be introduced in this section, so let's buckle down and get to it!

You completed the very first step toward optimizing your job feed in the last chapter. Having a profile that is 100% complete, verified, and accurate to the job type you're looking for will drastically streamline your search for those jobs. Upwork has a vested interest in matching clients with high-quality freelancers. Those who align themselves most closely with how Upwork has designed the platform will see the most significant benefit in finding jobs. Creating an impressive profile does precisely that.

How to Use Search Filters to Find the Perfect Job

There are a few significant areas where you can adjust the jobs you're looking at, though. The first is the search bar, where you can search by keywords *or* by skill sets. If you don't want to miss out on projects in your skill area but aren't sure of which search terms will flush out all of the jobs, you can quickly sweep available contracts for opportunities in that manner. This is why understanding the information in the previous chapters was so important: exhaustively searching the skillsets section when you built your profile has already informed you of how Upwork classifies you. Now, you can just access the jobs list for what you want.

Using only keywords or specific skills will cast a wide net, and you can narrow this by using an extensive set of filters. To begin, type any keyword into the search bar and hit "Enter."

The page that appears will give you a few options. The first is the "U.S. only" toggle switch. Clients can restrict jobs to only U.S. applicants for various reasons, which generally decreases overall competition and increases pay rates. Upwork states that US-only jobs tend to pay 75 percent more, but if you haven't verified your U.S. address, you won't see these. Once your profile is verified, however, you become eligible for this filter.

Next, you'll see a button titled "Filters." Click on that, and this expanded view is what you'll see. Play around with these until you feel comfortable with them, then really begin to dial into what kind of jobs are available. Which filters produce posts that catch your eye? Save the ones you find by marking the green heart icon. We'll use this later as we build your profile and show you how to integrate posting norms on Upwork into your profile--this is really just search engine optimization (SEO) for Upwork's search tools.

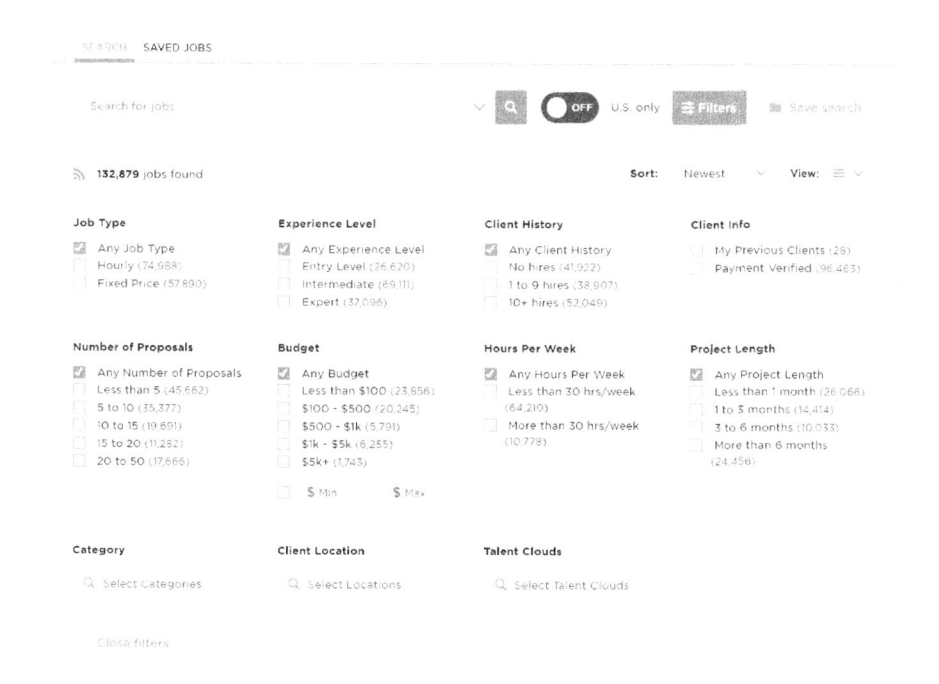

This is also an excellent way to gather information about how popular jobs are, what they are going for on the freelancer job market, whether they're primarily long or short-term gigs, et cetera. Work through each of the filter areas and explore. Before I let you loose, though, there are a few essential notes I need to make.

Job type. The first column is Job Type, and earlier I discussed how you should strive for a balance between fixed-price and hourly. Early on in your Upwork career, you'll likely find that you win a higher proportion of one or the other, depending on the industry. Don't let this panic you--it's very typical. After you get to 10 or 15 closed contracts, you'll want to begin making an effort to balance things out. Remember when we went through the client-side search options? They can also filter freelancers for various experience levels, and an imbalanced profile will result in fewer job matches than could have happened.

Job Type

- [x] Any Job Type
- [ ] Hourly (74,988)
- [ ] Fixed Price (57,890)

Experience level. The next option sorts jobs by experience level. This is mostly subjective--how would you rate your experience and quality of work? The most important aspect of this is brutal honesty with yourself. Some people have low self-esteem and would never consider themselves experts in a field, even if everyone around recognizes them as such. If this is you, it's a shortcoming you need to master. If you don't accurately value yourself, you're going to have a subpar experience as a freelancer and fail to be as successful as you could have been. Don't worry, this isn't something you have to overcome today, but you need to pay attention to it and slowly work toward an accurate self-valuation.

You don't have to put a ton of pressure on yourself to accurately gauge this at the outset if you're doing this part-time. This isn't your primary source of income, so you have time to focus on building that solid feedback reputation. Estimate where you think you should be, then begin looking at jobs one level lower than that. This allows you to bid on contracts that you're more likely to be overqualified for, and that gives you a higher chance of being able to knock it out of the park. Do that, you'll get killer feedback, and you're on your journey to success.

On the other side of the spectrum, if you overvalue yourself and then underperform, your feedback will reflect that. There is no quicker exit from an otherwise-promising Upwork career than to gain a bad reputation. Jobs that require higher expertise do pay more, and they're very tempting, but remember that feedback and a high Job Success Score comprise the path to a long, profitable association with Upwork.

If they seem far too easy, you can move things up a notch. Just make sure that you're doing it because you can legitimately handle more, and not because it's an ego thing.

Experience Level

- ☑ Any Experience Level
- ☐ Entry Level (26,620)
- ☐ Intermediate (69,111)
- ☐ Expert (37,096)

Critiquing an Ad

In Chapter Two, I taught you about the anatomy of an ad. You learned what each field was, what it meant, and how it connected to various search features. In this section, I'll break down what these fields communicate and how you can use them to find the right contracts.

Client history. The Client History section offers some fascinating insight into the contract mix. Approximately one-third of job postings come from clients with no experience on Upwork. This is something you need to pay attention to when bidding for three reasons. First, it's important to note that brand-new clients could be absolutely phenomenal, undeniably terrible, or anywhere in-between. You simply don't know at this point, because they haven't hired anyone. Upwork hasn't had a chance to measure that yet.

The site does a phenomenal job attracting high-quality clients, retaining them, and culling poor clients very quickly. However, the majority of those culls happen after the first couple of contracts. Although still small, you'll see a higher proportion of not-so-great clients in this pool, and you don't know which are which. Some of my best clients have been first-time clients, so don't shy away from this pool, just realize what the unknowns are.

In that spirit, if you've had a bad first experience with a client, check their job history. You can track their profile by going to My Jobs > All Contracts, locate the right one, then click on it and go to the original job posting. Scroll down, and you can see where you were in the client's job history, even if it's been a while. Upwork locks the feedback in chronological order; if your lousy experience came in the client's first three contracts, you probably didn't get a good indication of what Upwork culture is truly like, so don't get discouraged.

The second thing to keep in mind is that clients with no job history on Upwork aren't fully bought into the platform yet. They think it might satisfy their needs, but they're not sure. They're testing the waters. Other freelancing platforms might be a better fit for a particular business's needs, and if they decide to leave for that, they haven't vested much interest in their presence. Sometimes a job post will be abandoned as the client looks elsewhere.

This can be troublesome if a contract goes badly: the client can drop negative feedback and walk away from Upwork entirely, leaving you with a poor review and no repercussions for them. I don't see this happen often, but it is something to be aware of. Again, simply know the various factors going into a negotiation setting.

There is a second edge to this sword, however, and it's a good one. If you give a client an excellent first experience, they'll likely come to you again--repeatedly. They might offer you additional work in the same field, or ask you if you can handle work in other areas. I've had clients ask me for help in using the platform to find other specialties; this is an excellent opportunity to positively mold their' expectations on Upwork cultural norms. For example, outlining the types of things they should ask for in the job posting, how to evaluate a freelancer's profile to find a winner, etc. You can do all this because you read this book, and you know Upwork Basics from the ground up.

Cultural norms are the third area to be aware of when pitching to clients who are new to the platform: they simply haven't had time to get used to what's typical for the Upwork environment. What are the standard rates at which they get quality freelancers? How much interaction should they ask for in the interview process? If they ask you for something outside the norm, try to gently bring them back in line with what is typical for Upwork in your experience. If a brand-new Upwork client tries to negotiate too hard, it's better to walk away than take the contract.

I also want you to notice the balance of clients who have moderate levels of experience on Upwork (1 to 9 hires) and those who have extensive experience (10 or more hires). There are more experienced contracts (39% of total) than there are those with moderate experience (29%) or even no experience (32%). Upwork does an excellent job of attracting and retaining high-quality clients.

Client History

- ☑ Any Client History
- ☐ No hires (41,922)
- ☐ 1 to 9 hires (38,907)
- ☐ 10+ hires (52,049)

Client info. This is a handy tool. If you've done an excellent job for someone, this is a great place to find repeat clients. If you've had a few rough experiences, you might want to double-check if a job is from a client you didn't get along with before submitting a bid.

Client Info
- [ ] My Previous Clients (28)
- [ ] Payment Verified (96,483)

Number of proposals. A couple of factors will immediately turn me off of a job possibility, and one of those is if it exceeds 10 proposals that have already been submitted. At that point, I think there's too much competition for me to stand out, and my chances of being hired have decreased, so I move on in my search.

The good news is that more than 60% of jobs fit in this criteria, so you're still retaining the lion's share of the posts while cutting out the lowest 40%

Number of Proposals
- [x] Any Number of Proposals
- [ ] Less than 5 (45,662)
- [ ] 5 to 10 (35,377)
- [ ] 10 to 15 (19,691)
- [ ] 15 to 20 (11,282)
- [ ] 20 to 50 (17,666)

Every minute I spend bidding for jobs instead of working them is a minute I'm not being paid, so I only want to go with high-quality shots. When you do this right, this is what your "My Stats" section looks like:

	Less often	More often
You were viewed		
You were interviewed		
You were hired		

Upwork compares how often you were viewed, interviewed, and hired compared to your peers in the same industry. This tells you whether your bidding strategies (starting with selecting the right contract) are working.

There were several reasons why Upwork decided to charge for connects, but the bottom line is that they wanted to decrease the number of bids submitted for each job, making each contract more selective. When people have to pay even a few cents to apply, they hesitate for a moment longer. This means that only the freelancers who feel they are genuinely qualified bid, creating a smaller pool of applicants where it's easier to stand out.

Budget. Don't put much stock in this feature for a few reasons. First and foremost, there is no commitment level associated with an estimated budget. Even with a confirmed payment method, a client does not have to deposit money into escrow until they hire someone for the job. While it's extremely rare for someone to be intentionally deceptive, it isn't uncommon for someone to fat finger a number, or more commonly, not know how to truly valuate a job. Use this as a relative indicator, but I've had jobs initially valued at a couple of hundred dollars turn into tens of thousands of dollars worth of work.

Budget

☑ Any Budget
☐ Less than $100 (23,856)
☐ $100 - $500 (20,245)
☐ $500 - $1k (5,791)
☐ $1k - $5k (6,255)
☐ $5k+ (1,743)

☐ $ Min $ Max

Unfortunately, you'll occasionally run into a client who is obviously overvaluing the job to get higher-value freelancers and will then offer them less. If this happens, don't take the contract. These clients are always headaches and will cause stress and almost always result in bad feedback for you.

Hours per week & project length. Take this category with a grain of salt, as well. Jobs often change from the first time the client conceives of it to final execution. Use this in the same way you did when setting your availability according to these categories: they're a relative indicator of time required, but not an absolute one by any means.

Hours Per Week

☑ Any Hours Per Week
☐ Less than 30 hrs/week (64,210)
☐ More than 30 hrs/week (10,778)

Project Length

☑ Any Project Length
☐ Less than 1 month (26,066)
☐ 1 to 3 months (14,414)
☐ 3 to 6 months (10,033)
☐ More than 6 months (24,456)

It's also not uncommon for a newer client to realize they incorrectly classified a job and need to switch it to a different type of payment (e.g., from hourly to fixed-price). As long as you both agree to it, that isn't a problem; that just means you shouldn't disregard all contracts based on the assumption that everything about the ad is accurate.

Category, client location, & talent clouds. The Category drop-down menu allows you to search for any major category or even specific subcategories of jobs. The Client Location menu is set at the country level, so it won't be of much use to freelancers in the United States but is very beneficial for international freelancers. Finally, the Talent Clouds I discussed earlier can be individually searched, so don't hesitate to check those out once you get accepted into one.

"Save search" button. Once you've spent some time building a search, you might want to save it. Click this button, then title the search accordingly. These will be located on the left side of your home screen in the Find Work section. I've got three saved: "Generic Writing Search," "Expert Writing," and "Expert Research." A single click will recall all of the search criteria and sort the available jobs appropriately.

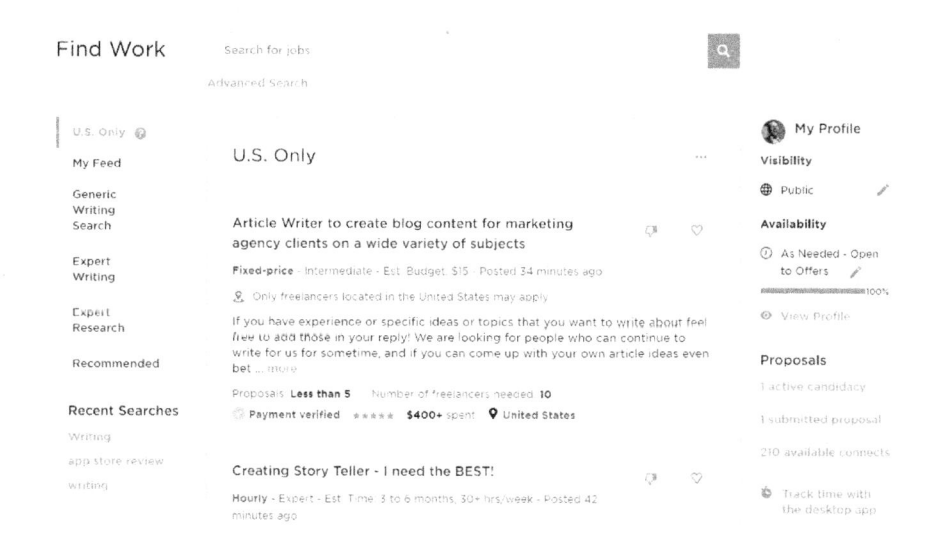

If your job feed ever seems stuck, and the top job is listed as being posted several hours before, clear the cache on your browser. Occasionally it will fail to refresh correctly, and you don't want to miss any jobs due to a glitch.

What to Look for in a Client

You'll frequently see a "Featured Job" tag on contracts that appear at or near the top of your job feed. These clients have paid a fee to push their contract to the top. This tells you several things. First, the client is invested--they've already spent money to make this happen.

Second, the client *really* wants this job filled. This is especially true if the job has been renewed (right above the location tag in the image below). That means the client has not only not hired anyone, but the client has tacitly rejected everyone who submitted a bid to that point. A renewal overrides my previous rule about submitted proposals because it effectively places the client's applicant pool down to 0. Even if you see 50 applicants, if it was renewed less than an hour ago, bid. Those first 50 applicants no longer count in the client's eyes.

Third, you have an edge in price negotiation. The client has paid money to feature this job, knowing how much they want it to be filled. They've been watching the situation closely, and have been dissatisfied with all proposals so far. They renewed the job posting, indicating this is a must-fill position. If the client extends a contract offer, you have quite a bit of power on your side of the table.

Use this wisely and respectfully. Remember that long-term success is created by developing a good name for yourself. Offer your services at a fair price, even if you have all of the leverage--just don't feel any pressure to go down in price. Ask what you're worth, and don't apologize for it.

🔷 **FEATURED JOB**

CCH Axcess Tax Support

Hourly - Expert - Est. Time: More than 6 months, 10-30 hrs/week - Renewed 51 minutes ago

📍 Only freelancers located in the United States may apply

We need a consultant who is expert in CCH Axcess Tax to be our support person. The support department at CCH is not very good. Most of our questions are simple, we have been using Axcess Tax for one year and are still new to the software.

User Research

Proposals: **Less than 5**

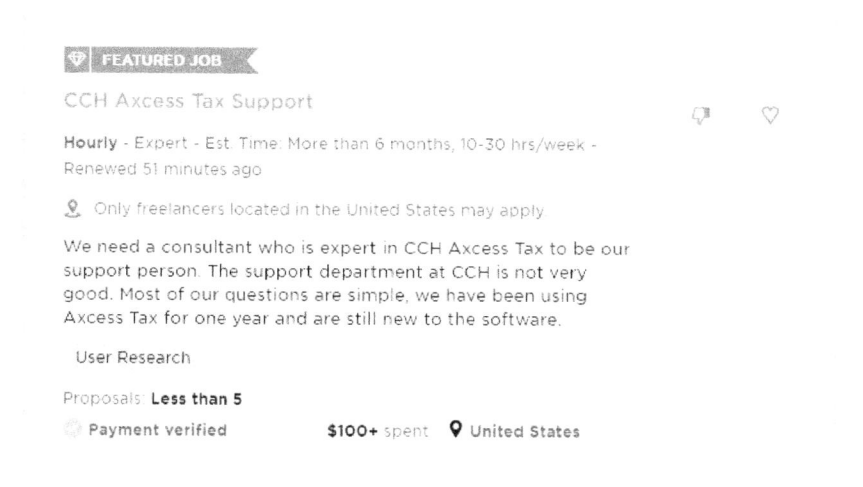

Payment verified $100+ spent   📍 United States

Evaluating a Job Posting

Title. The title of a job posting varies in how valuable the information is. Some clients write unambiguous titles that clearly communicate what they're looking for, while others can be a bit vague. Because each of these is custom-written by the client, there is a lot of room for typos to wreak havoc. Even if you have an excellent set of saved searches, it's good practice to review the entire job feed for your primary freelancing occupation at least once a day.

An ideal title will tell you what kind of freelancer the client is looking for (check for keywords such as "writer," "programmer," or "developer") as well as the type of work to be done (such as "10 Responsive Email Templates" or "WordPress shopping cart set up"). Even if the title is well-worded, you should read the entire description field for several reasons.

First, Upwork allows clients to reuse templates, and occasionally a job posting will slip through with a title for Contract A, but content for Contract B--and these can be in entirely different fields.

Occasionally clients need help determining precisely what they want; one of the most common reasons to hire freelancers is because clients don't know how to do the specific tasks themselves; as a result, they might ask the wrong questions or describe the work incorrectly upfront. Reading through the description field will help you know if the client accurately described the work to be done or needs a bit of help fleshing out the details.

Finally, it isn't uncommon for a client to place a requirement in the job ad itself that you must address to be considered. Sometimes it's a very specific question; e.g., "Tell me specifically about your last job in X." Occasionally, the client will say, "Put (some random word) at the top of your cover letter, so I know you read it." Even if you're a perfect match for the job, you'll miss this if you don't read the ad thoroughly, and that will likely mean missing out on the job itself.

Timelines. The very first thing you should look for when reviewing job posts is the time it was posted.

Script writer

Scriptwriting
Posted 16 minutes ago

Submit a Proposal

♡ Save Job

⚑ Flag as inappropriate

Never bid on a job that was posted more than 24 hours prior. In the corporate world, a job can take three to six months from the time the need is identified until it is posted, candidates are interviewed, hired, onboarded, and begin work. The average timeline for Upwork, however, is 72 hours. This can be broken down roughly into the following three areas:

- First 24 hours: Job is posted, bids are solicited, and client narrows candidate field
- Second 24 hours: Interviews begin with candidates
- Final 24 hours: Candidate is selected, and work begins

Obviously, this can vary quite a bit, but this is the case more often than not. After the first 24 hours, your chances of winning a bid decrease substantially--and you still have to pay the same price for connects. If you find a job that seems perfectly suited to your skill set and experience, you can bid on it, of course. However, remember that the client may be in the interview stage, so you're going to be competing for a first look against freelancers who have already been identified as potential winners.

What you should know about renewed jobs. One exception to this is jobs that are renewed, as I mentioned above. Upwork has a phenomenally varied field of freelancers, but occasionally a job is so specifically targeted that a client can't find the perfect match they're looking for. In this situation, a client can renew a job that's more than 72 hours old to bump the job posting back to the top of the list.

> Looking for high quality short reports
>
> Fixed-price - Intermediate - Est. Budget: $100 - Renewed 58 minutes ago
>
> Only freelancers located in the United States may apply.
>
> Please, only bid if you can produce high quality content FAST. I'll need the first report by Sept 5, 2019. I am looking for a new valuable, consistent writer to produce original content reports/short stories for my website. I'm looking to build a lo ... more
>
> eBooks   Research   Comedy   Fiction   Humor
>
> Proposals: **Less than 5**
>
> Payment verified $0 spent   United States

A renewed job posting can tell you several things. As I just mentioned, it could simply be due to an extremely specific job posting that isn't easy to match--if that's the case, you should be able to tell by the wording of the ad. However, several potentially negative things could cause a contract to fail to attract a high-quality freelancer pool.

Sometimes clients post work at such a cut rate that no competent freelancer would bid on it. Be sure to evaluate the work description thoroughly and know that you can bid a fair price. Another reason freelancers might refuse to submit bids is that the client's feedback rating is very poor. Upwork does an excellent job attracting a high-quality pool of clients, but as with every group of people, you'll eventually run into a bad apple. To avoid being trapped in a contract with a client who can't be pleased, always check their feedback ratings and comments.

Upwork reviews work on a five-star system like Amazon product ratings, but it's essential to understand the cultural nuances behind how an organization uses rating systems. At Upwork, the default assumption is that if the freelancer and client each perform according to expectations, five stars should be awarded. That's not an "above and beyond" rating, but rather a default for timely, quality work that met expectations from the freelancer side, and clear expectations, prompt communication, and painless payment for a client. Knowing this is critical because a client with a 3-star average rating is anything but average--this is someone you should actively avoid.

You should also dig more deeply than just the ratings and at least peruse the feedback comments left by previous freelancers who worked with this client. A client can have a 4.95 rating across 30 contracts, but as you look at his history, you might find that 29 of those were for easy contracts that didn't require much effort (e.g., reviewing a product on Amazon or an app in the App store) and only one required real work. If that "real work" contract has a terrible review from the freelancer, it's a sign that you should probably be cautious.

I've had two clients like this. One owned a dating app and had hired literally thousands of freelancers to give app reviews. I was hired as part of a five-member writing team with an editor, and after a couple of weeks, none of us were working for him and had all agreed that he was one of the worst clients we'd encountered. Another client would target clients who were early in their careers and trying to earn good feedback. He'd advertise a job at a specific price, then cut the rate with each successive milestone until the freelancer decided to end the contract. At that point, he'd tell them how badly a poor review from him would affect them. He'd only give them a good review if they gave him a five-star rating.

Upwork generally does an excellent job of rapidly culling bad clients, so each of these instances is relatively rare, but still possible. Your goal should always be to do everything possible to create and maintain good working relationships with your clients. Upwork provides a filter to search specifically for clients with whom you've previously worked.

U.S. only   Filters   Save search

Sort: Newest   ∨   View: ≡ ∨

Client Info

☐ My Previous Clients (8)
☐ Payment Verified (21,481)

This can also work well if you've had a bad experience with a client and specifically want to avoid him or her.

Evaluating the "About the client" Section

You'll find a brief discussion about this in Chapter Two, where the focus is more on understanding an ad's anatomy.

Payment method verified. The first thing you notice in this section is whether the client has a validated method of payment on record. Upwork makes finances easy for everyone involved: they bill the client and then handle transferring payment to you. When a client creates an account, they are prompted to list a debit or credit card. Because this isn't required to post an ad, Upwork will allow an employer to post a job ad without confirming a payment source, but this should always cause you to step back in caution for a moment.

About the client

⊙ **Payment method verified**

★★★★★ 5.00 of 2 reviews

United States
Tacoma 04:15 pm

8 jobs posted
38% hire rate, 1 open job

$1k+ total spent
3 hires, 1 active

$15.00/hr avg hourly rate paid
8 hours

Member since Mar 15, 2016

Time zone. You can also see the client's time zone. This matters more for some kinds of projects than others. The majority of freelance work doesn't require a particular location. If you're involved with anything that requires regular working hours, standard collaboration times, or connecting with the client throughout their workday, you're going to want to be in the same or a directly adjacent time zone.

Jobs posted & hire rate. The "jobs posted" and "hire rate" will give you an indication of whether this client is fishing, hiring off-platform, or hiring on-platform. Someone who is fishing will have posted multiple jobs but will have a low hire rate. He'll post job ads to research what's available, and then might never follow up with any of the applicants, which could indicate you're wasting your time. Consider the following client:

About the client

Payment method verified

United States
Hawthorne 04:33 pm

3 jobs posted
0% hire rate, 3 open jobs

Member since Aug 22, 2016

He's been a member of the Upwork community for four years but has never once hired anyone on the platform. If the type of job you're looking at is a short-term, fixed-price task, he's fishing--I wouldn't waste my time applying. However, in this case, the kind of job he's advertising is a long-term, hourly position, which indicates that he might be trying to hire off-platform. This means he's using Upwork like a job board and might ask you to come work directly for him without any intention of awarding the contract here.

I will say that I've known a few people who have successfully met long-term employers this way, but I would recommend against it. Going off-platform not only surrenders all of the protections you have as a freelancer, but it also violates Upworks terms and conditions, which could have severe repercussions for you. If you decide to do this, just beware of the price it may cost and the connotations it will have.

If the hire rate is above 50 percent, you can safely assume that this is a genuine client interested in hiring on-platform. Don't be discouraged if it isn't much higher than that; sometimes, clients are involved in incredibly niche industries and looking for extremely specific matches they can't always find. They might be very earnest about hiring someone; it's just relatively common for them not to find precisely what they're looking for. That isn't an issue.

Member since ____. The final piece of this section is how long a client has been part of the Upwork community. This is largely irrelevant since someone could have joined three months ago and gone whole-hog on the operation, posting 50 jobs and hiring on 40 of them. On the other hand, they could be like the fellow above, who's been on the platform for four years and has never hired anyone. It's a data point, but generally isn't a reason to decide for or against applying for a job.

○ **Less than 30 hrs/week**
Hourly

▭ **More than 6 months**
Project Length

♀ **Expert**
I am willing to pay higher rates for the most experienced freelancers

⏱ **$15.00-$29.00**
Hourly

Job type. This is the cross-section for a job that's described as hourly instead of fixed-price. The client can specify a number of things here. The first is approximately how many hours she thinks it will take up each week, and the options are "less than 30 hrs/week," "more than 30 hrs/week," and "To be determined." Keep in mind that this is an estimate; while it is likely relatively close, there's no guarantee that it's accurate.

Job length. Second, you'll see how long a client estimates the job will last. There are four choices she can select from: less than 1 month, 1 to 3 months, 3 to 6 months, and more than 6 months. Again, keep in mind that this is an indicator, nothing more. While the vast majority of clients do their best to represent the job accurately, it isn't uncommon for them to be advertising for a new or evolving role, and they're just estimating. Less commonly, but still something to be aware of, some clients will attempt to make a job seem as appealing as possible (e.g., long-term, high pay) to get higher quality freelancers.

Pay range. There's an hourly range listed in the bottom left of this section, and this is something you should pay attention to. When a client creates a job ad, Upwork leads them through a pretty extensive set of questions digging into the specific type of work they want and skill sets a freelancer will need. By the time they reach the payment rate screen, Upwork has a pretty good idea of what that talent will cost, and they recommend an hourly range based on what this type of work typically goes for on the platform. The client can choose to keep that range or override it with one that more accuratcly reflects their budget. There's always the possibility that the client just clicks through this stage and doesn't pay attention, but it's far more likely that they see this budget range as indicative of what they're willing to pay. If the high end is less than you're willing to work for, moving on is your best bet; otherwise, you're likely wasting your time by bidding.

Budgets. When a client selects a fixed-price rather than an hourly model, they're asked to put in the specific budget amount. You'll see one of two types of responses. The first is $5, which is the minimum a job can go for. In this case, the client usually has no idea what the job will cost, and they want you to bid what you think you should be paid. If this happens, feel free to bid very accurately, but you also need to explicitly explain where that quoted price comes from and what it's based on. You're going to be competing with other freelancers who will try to get in by lowballing. Quality clients aren't afraid to pay what you're worth, but they need to understand the price tag before signing off on it.

If the estimated budget is higher than $5, they're likely putting down what they think the job is worth or what they can afford to pay. That doesn't mean you're limited to that; a fair number of the fixed-price jobs I've won have exceeded the budget as it was listed on the original job posting. In one instance, I was able to justify my bid that was five times what the job was posted for (although this is definitely an exception). This is where you need to be a salesperson, though: pitch what it will cost, then justify it.

Retainers. Upwork just introduced a new type of billing model that revolves around a weekly retainer. The client will pay you a set amount to remain continuously available, and you'll both agree on an hourly rate that will function similar to an hourly contract. Presumably, the client will pay a slightly lower hourly rate because they have you on retainer, but that's up to you to negotiate.

Experience level. Finally, the client will estimate the experience level she thinks she needs. Take this with a grain of salt, and compare it to how extensively the client has hired on Upwork, as shown in the "About the client" section. Many people who are either new to the platform or do a lot of international hiring will list that they want an expert and then offer a ceiling rate that's one-third of what experts in that field typically charge on Upwork. Occasionally, a client is willing to pay very high prices but will list that they only need a freelancer working at an intermediate level. Keep this in mind when you're using filters for searches.

Geographic preferences. Clients can set certain geographic limitations or preferences for freelancers. They can specify that they only want freelancers in the U.S., and they can get even more specific and require a particular time zone or zip code. If you live in the U.S., you can click an option on your home feed to limit what you see to "U.S. Only" jobs. On average, these jobs pay rates that are 75 percent higher, have 20 percent less competition, and the overall contract size is 50 percent greater than what you'll find on Upwork international markets. There's really no reason to go outside of U.S. Only jobs if you're eligible for them.

PRO TIP

If you're not located in the U.S., consider finding an agency that's headquartered in the U.S. Since contracts are awarded to the agency, and they can subcontract the work to you, this is a potential door for more lucrative work.

When a client has limited a contract location to a city or time zone, they may or may not be strict about it. I've been hired nearly a dozen times for jobs that were initially location limited to a specific time zone I was outside of, but a good fit for the project. Read the ad content and make your best judgment call on whether the work would require you to be where the client has listed; if not, submit a bid and explain why you could still complete the requirements where you're located.

Understanding Service Fees

Upwork's major moneymaker comes in the form of charging service fees, which are essentially commissions on each dollar earned by a freelancer. The typical model consists of three tiers:

- 20 percent for the first $500 billed with a client
- 10 percent for client billings between $500.01 and $10,000
- 5 percent for client billings over $10,000

These are charged per client, not per contract. If you have two consecutive contracts with a particular client and the first one ends at $499, the next job will pick up at the $500 mark, so you don't reset. While these seem steep (and I agree that they are), they're offset by two realities. First, Upwork wants to encourage long-term relationship building between clients and freelancers, so this financial model is just one of several mechanisms that reinforces this. Second, it's easier to justify higher pay rates when you explain to a client that 20 percent of your initial fees go straight to Upwork. As the contract continues, you'll end up keeping more of what you earn.

This is the typical model, but there are exceptions. Upwork Plus clients can negotiate different rates with Upwork that will cause these fees to vary. One client I work with periodically has a flat 10 percent service fee for all contracts. That's great for all new freelance hires, but it can cost quite a bit if you work for them long-term. You don't get any say in this from the contractor's perspective, but it is something to be aware of, particularly when you're setting and negotiating your rates.

Sales tax. Upwork just started collecting state sales tax for clients who live in Connecticut, Massachusetts, New York, Ohio,

Pennsylvania, and Texas. Check the Upwork Community for updates on this and if the list of states expands. The good news is that this makes it simpler at tax time. The bad news is, well... it's taxes.

Chapter Four Exercise

Using searches well is going to make a night and day difference in your Upwork career. This exercise consists of two different tasks that will set you up for success.

Using filters. I want you to use search filters to find the following list of jobs. Search in the specific area you want to work--these are jobs you could potentially bid for. Screenshot and save them to a folder. Compare each of these with the others you find in this checklist and see if you can spot differences you missed before.

- Find 2 jobs that are Hourly, 2 that are Fixed Price, and 2 that are Weekly Retainer.
- Find 2 jobs at an Entry level, 2 at an Intermediate level, and 2 at an Expert level.
- Find 1 job ad for a client with no hires, 1 job ad for a client with 25 or fewer hires, and 1 job ad for a client with 100 or more hires.
- Find 1 job with 0 proposals, 1 job with 10 to 15 proposals, and 1 job with 20 to 50 proposals.
- Find 2 jobs with $5 budgets, 2 jobs with a $500 - $1k budget, and 2 jobs with a $5k+ budget.
- Find 2 jobs listed at "less than 30 hours per week" and 2 at "more than 30 hours per week."
- Find 2 jobs for each of the categories in the "Project Length" filter.

Saving searches. After you've worked through all of these filters, you should have a good idea of what kinds of jobs are available with different combinations. Open the folder where you have your screenshots, then open a browser and go to an advanced Upwork search. Work through all of your screenshots to find a combination that pulls the specific types of jobs you're looking for.

Once you've put everything in, hit the "Save Search" button in the top right corner. Name it appropriately, then repeat the process once more. You should have a minimum of two saved searches that you can quickly run. I have one for "Writing" and one for "Research"; between these and my home feed, I typically find all of the jobs I need.

CHAPTER FIVE

Placing a Winning Bid

Bidding is the lifeblood of independent contracting, and Upwork has its own unique flavor and culture. Understanding how bidding works and using best practices to your advantage can make all the difference between a successful experience and one where you throw in the towel.

I've coached numerous freelancers over the past few years, and bidding is the single most common area of frustration. Work through this section carefully: highlight it, mark it up, and revisit it often until you're consistently winning the contracts you want.

The Material for Your Cover Letter

You'll rarely use a resume on the Upwork platform. Certain types of jobs (e.g., administrative assistant) will still reference these occasionally, but they tend to be exceptions. Instead, what you'll be using to apply for literally every single position is a cover letter.

Custom-writing a cover letter for each bid gives you a much higher chance at winning that contract, but it can also take an absurd amount of time. This is especially true if you're not a writer. On the other hand, using a prewritten letter saves a tremendous amount of time, but it can come across as less than authentic. Many clients explicitly state that using a copy/paste cover letter will cause them to disregard your application immediately.

The best solution is a hybrid approach that maximizes the convenience of a prewritten cover letter and the personality of a customized statement. The way you do that is relatively straightforward. First, create an extensive list--and by "extensive," I mean "all-encompassing"--of all of your job experiences, unique life experiences, and interests. You're going to develop a paragraph for every significant experience you've had, every skill set you could possibly advertise, and every hobby that might land you a job.

This goes far beyond what you list on a resume. You'll find ads for the most bizarre types of jobs, including clients who are conducting market research and simply want to ask an experienced hobbyist some questions about what they prefer. Do you knit, tie flies for fishing, or enjoy smoking pot? Have you had unique experiences, like visiting all fifty states or spending a month as a whitewater rafting guide at the Grand Canyon? At some point, you'll find job postings seeking people with these interests or experiences. My favorite analogy to use about freelancing is that there are the number and variety of jobs you'd expect to find on Craigslist combined with the professionalism of LinkedIn.

Drafting a Master Cover Letter

Once you have that list, draft a paragraph on each bullet you've written down. Don't be too hard on your English at this point; you're mainly concerned with getting thoughts down on paper. Freelancing tends to be relatively casual and very conversational, so I want you to adjust the mental image you most likely have in your mind. When most people write resumes, they imagine a stern businessman in a suit and tie whose posture is so ramrod straight you wonder if he has an actual stick up his ass. In all of my interviews, I've never encountered someone wearing a tie. Not once. Talking with someone in board shorts sitting in their kitchen, however, well... that's happened a few times.

Don't be so casual that you come across as talking with a friend, but if you write like you're drafting this for the best boss you've ever had after working for him or her for five years, you'll nail the tone pretty well. Respectful but casual is how I'd describe the perfect balance. Focus on telling your story as a unique human being more than trying to come across as a flawless, cookie-cutter clone of a stereotypical office professional.

Here are three paragraphs from my cover letter master:

> *I have an extensive and varied body of research experience. A previous research client wanted me to look into computer repair contracts for military service academies. Due to the unique combination of higher education, the federal government, and the military, she had tried for months on her own and had been stonewalled at every turn. Within a few days, I provided her information about who held each contract and where each one was in its life cycle. I then used an exclusive source to outline all the steps she would need to win the next round of bids, including contact information for each contract official and the terms of the current winning bids. In her words, she was "blown away."*
>
> *I've published multiple books as a ghostwriter in a variety of subjects, including two Amazon bestsellers. My clients will occasionally ask me to write with their voice, and I've*

> *been very successful at imitating someone's writing and speaking style, down to unique colloquialisms and idioms. I love when I am given the freedom of expression to weave a client's story for them, however; after I finished a recent book, the client told me that the manuscript (which was a motivational, self-help work) motivated HIM after reading it!*
>
> *I've written copy for more than 40 websites in a variety of subject areas, and my work is of such high quality that my clients almost always become repeat customers. The subject matter is across the board (I've written about neurology, cannabis legalization, and macroeconomics in a single afternoon). The style has been everything from sales copy to research writing to personal storytelling. Clients have repeatedly told me that I have a unique ability to reach out to readers and pull them in.*

In high school or college English class, you were taught to focus on a cohesive flow while smoothly transitioning from the end of one paragraph to the beginning of the next. Yeah, forget all that. In the cover letter style we're using, you want each paragraph to be able to stand by itself and have no reference to the one before and after it. Once you're done, you should be able to copy and paste paragraphs from anywhere in your Word doc and drop them anywhere else without making it better or worse.

You're not so much creating a cover letter in this document as you are putting together a bunch of building blocks. This is your Job Application Toolbox (JAT), and you don't care if the hammer sits to the left or right of the screwdriver.

The Final Paragraph

Now, focus on the very last paragraph. This is where you wrap up your pitch and focus on your work ethic, style, and what you bring to the table. Here's mine:

> *I would love to work with you on this project. As I state on my profile, my primary goal is ensuring that you get precisely what you want. Whenever I complete a job, I always ask my clients if I've done everything possible to earn a five-star rating. My favorite response so far has been: "Can I give you six?" That's the kind of quality I provide. Please don't hesitate to reach out with any questions and I'll be more than happy to answer them for you!*
>
> *Respectfully,*
> *Josh*

Boom. Short, sweet, simple, and ends on a positive note. If you want to be even more efficient, go ahead and create prewritten cover letters for different focus areas of your work. For example, I have one for general writing, one for research, and one for project management. I keep all of my paragraphs in a master cover letter, then just copy and paste the ones that apply to research into that letter so I have to do even less hunting and editing when a research opportunity becomes available. Let's say my master cover letter has ten paragraphs, and 2, 4, 6, and 7 apply to research. Rather than pull up the master each time and then individually copy and paste those four paragraphs, I just save 2, 4, 6, and 7 into a research letter.

Nailing the Intro Paragraph

Here's how you're going to use your cover letter: when you look for job ads, pull this humongous document up and keep it in the background. If you find one you like, click on "Submit a Proposal" and go to the Cover Letter section.

The very first paragraph of each letter is one you'll custom write for that job proposal. It doesn't have to be extensive; 90 percent of mine end up maxing out at three sentences. The goal of this paragraph is to connect with the client and let him or her know that you're a real person who cares, you've read the ad, and you legitimately think you'll be a good fit. Nothing will turn an employer off more quickly than thinking you're spamming job postings, applying to every single one that you're even remotely qualified for. (Hell, maybe you are, but do it the right way.) If clients include their names on the job post, use it.

These first two sentences will determine whether a client reads any of the rest of your cover letter or even glances at the work samples you've attached. Here are some of my most recent ones:

> Hi Kim,
>
> I'm intrigued by your story, and I think I might be able to help. I'm an experienced, published ghostwriter and storyteller who excels at eliciting specific emotions from an audience. I can pull readers in and captivate them, driving the effects you want your story to have.
>
> Hello!
>
> I think I would be an excellent fit for your job. I'm a military veteran (seven years active duty Air Force, four years reserves), and one of my assignments required extensive interview experience over a three-year period. I'm a

creative writer who can elicit targeted reactions with my work. You'll find three samples attached, each focused on different emotions.

Hi there!

I think I would be an awesome fit for your job. I live in Oregon and am a huge cannabis fan. As a freelancer, I've written about multiple aspects of weed, from legalization to its effects to the lifestyle. I wrote the feature article for the premier edition of Cannabis Packaging News magazine, which was well-received.

Each one of these cover letters resulted in an interview. The clients knew that I'd read their job posting, evaluated it against my experience, and genuinely believed I could give them exactly what they wanted.

Plug and Play from the JAT

OK, you've written your first couple of sentences; now, it's time to plug and play. Pull up your JAT and then copy and paste whatever paragraphs apply to that particular job posting. Unlike what most conversations in your high school locker room revolved around, length doesn't really matter here. A client doesn't want to read unnecessary information any more than you enjoyed writing it. A good cover letter will have a minimum of three paragraphs:

- The customized introduction
- At least one copy/paste from your JAT that describes some kind of applicable experience
- Your killer summary that woos the client far better than Romeo did Juliet (hopefully your jobs end up much better than that story did)

Once it's all put together in the text box on the job posting, read through it. You might want to add a few words here or there to tie things together, or tweak some of the sentences in your JAT paragraphs to make it more applicable to that job posting. I can't stress this review enough. Eventually, you'll find something huge that you missed when you put it all together, like your summary paragraph (I've done it more than once).

When you're satisfied, copy the entire body of the text and drop it into a blank Word doc. You don't have to save the doc, you just want that unique cover letter to exist somewhere else until you submit it. There have been several occasions when I bumped a keyboard shortcut or accidentally clicked on the wrong spot on my browser and closed the application window; if you hadn't dropped that text elsewhere, you've got to go back and recreate it from scratch. Shy of biting into an over-microwaved Hot Pocket or pulling a nose hair, nothing will bring angry tears to your eyes more quickly, so it's best just to avoid the situation with a quick copy/paste.

Using Work Samples

At this point, you typically want to include some work samples, depending on the nature of the job. How much you add really depends on several factors. If you're in a visual field, more is better. A client can rapidly click through the attachments and get a full-spectrum appreciation of your work. If you work in an arena that centers around back-end development, you might not include anything at all and simply rely on descriptions of what you can do and reference client feedback.

PRO TIP

"What do you do if you don't have any work samples?" The first thing you should do is ask yourself if any personal projects would fit the bill. When I began writing, I didn't have any samples a client had commissioned, so I pulled several entries from my blog. If you're a web developer, a graphic designer, or any one of a number of other specialties, you've probably played around with your skillset and can use some of those as work samples.

However, if you genuinely don't have anything, consider making one up. It's labor-intensive at the start, but it will be a huge boost for you. Here's the best way to get started: find an ideal job on Upwork with very clear deliverables, complete the first part of the project, and submit it with your cover letter. Upwork's terms and conditions prohibit clients from asking for free work, but they don't restrict you from voluntarily completing free work to get the job, particularly if you're just using this as an opportunity to build up your work sample library. Clients will be impressed at how closely your example aligns with their requirements ("Oh my, what a coincidence!"), and you're that much more likely to be awarded the contract.

For many freelancing areas, such as writing (my bread and butter), you have to be judicious about what to include. If you have a work sample that is a perfect match for what that client is looking for, attach that one and leave it at that. If you have several that are close, include up to three. Very rarely will I include more than three, and as someone who has hired hundreds of freelancers, I can say with absolute certainty that less is more. Remember that your application isn't the only one I'm looking at. If I see six attachments on your response, I'm either going to randomly pick one (and it might not be the one you think is best), or I'm going to get irritated by having to open so many, driving down the chances that I'll hire you. The more care you put into selecting specifically targeted samples of work, the higher your chances of being hired are. The more haphazardly you toss attachments onto the pile, the more your prospects plummet like a skydiver with an unopened parachute.

Responding to Invitations

When a client invites you to a job, you'll get a customized invitation at the bottom of the screen that looks something like this:

> Original message from client
>
> Hello!
>
> I'd like to invite you to take a look at the job I've posted. Please submit a proposal if you're available and interested.
>
> Joseph U.

This message is the default text that Upwork provides. If it varies from this at all, you know that the client typed it explicitly, adding further weight to the fact that he or she invited you. The application process is nearly identical to finding jobs on your own with three small, but crucial differences.

First, you know the client's first name from the message. Instead of starting your cover letter off with a generic "Hello!" you can include his name. "Hi, Joseph" is warmer, more intimate, and helps to establish rapport immediately. Always use the client's name in the intro to your cover letter when you're invited to a job.

Second, invitations don't cost any connects when you apply to them. They're free opportunities to earn work, so there's no harm in submitting a bid if you have time. This also makes them the perfect opportunity to escalate your pay rate if you've got a full workload. Let's say you've got 35 hours of work at $40 an hour and are ready to move up. Don't be afraid to submit a bid for $55 an hour. The worst they can do is say no, it doesn't cost you a cent, and you could get a much more lucrative deal out of it.

Finally, the client found *you*. That means you've already got one foot in the door. The moment you respond, your bid doesn't go into the queue with everyone else's--it gets delivered straight to the client's inbox. They will see your proposal, so your chances of being noticed are 100 percent, and the possibility of you winning the contract substantially increases.

Handling Screening Questions

When clients create a job post on Upwork, they have the option to include up to five additional screening questions. They can choose to write their own or choose from ten generic questions that are available:

- Do you have any questions about the job description?
- Do you have suggestions to make this project run successfully?
- What challenging part of this job are you most experienced in?
- What part of this project most appeals to you?
- What past project or job have you had that is most like this one and why?
- What questions do you have about the project?
- Which of the required job skills do you feel you are strongest at?
- Which part of this project do you think will take the most time?
- Why did you apply to this particular job?
- Why do you think you are a good fit for this particular project?

Generic screening questions are one of my least favorite aspects of the Upwork platform. The majority of clients who opt to include them are newer clients who aren't very familiar with the platform, and the way they're used in the selection process is inconsistent. Some clients all but ignore the cover letter in favor of the information in these text boxes, while others begin to ignore the text box responses after they review three or four bids and realize how tedious they are to work through.

Generic screening you're caught in a bit of a catch-22. If you put all of the information in the screening questions and those end up being ignored, your chances of winning the contract diminish. If you put all of your cards in the cover letter and the client focuses on the additional questions, you're sunk. If you put everything in both places, you could irritate the client by being redundant. There's a very narrow road to effectively navigate this situation while maintaining the highest chance of winning the job regardless of who is sitting behind the other side of the screen and what questions they ask.

How you approach screening questions varies based on how they're included in the ad, so here are a few guidelines to follow. Deviate from them whenever you feel it's necessary, but following these will give you the most efficient bang for your buck.

First, if a client has taken the time to create an individualized question, whatever they ask is important to them and likely a hinge-point for the job. You should draft a customized response and answer what they're asking in a detailed fashion. You can (and should) refer to additional information included in your cover letter, but whatever you include in this response should be written as a specific response to this question.

Default Responses

If a client selects prepared questions from the list above, write a one-sentence response that refers back to the information in your cover letter. Here is how you should answer the following questions:

> **1. Do you have any questions about the job description?**
> Asking a clarifying question always demonstrates engagement

with the post, which is the purpose of the custom-written first paragraph in your cover letter. This question was added because many freelancers don't do that. If you have a question, ask it here. However, it's pretty common not to have any questions, particularly if the job posting was short on details. In this case, write some variation of "Not at this time. Your job description seemed very clear."

Don't feel pressure to come up with a question you didn't have just because they asked for it. Remember, the client didn't feel enough pressure to come up with a question of their own and just clicked an option box to make this appear, so they're not expecting a graduate thesis as a response.

2. **Do you have suggestions to make this project run successfully?** This can be an excellent opportunity to showcase your experience by saying something like: "In previous projects, I've found that X is a crucial step and makes everything at Y much easier." Be careful with your responses, though, and follow these three rules:

   A. Keep all comments optimistic. It's easy to come across as a Negative Nancy, and you want to avoid this connotation. The question specifically asked about making the project run successfully, not how to avoid making it unsuccessful.

   B. Keep all responses positive. This means focusing exclusively on things you *should* do, and never on things you *shouldn't* do. Remember that the client is posting this job because he needs help with something, which implies you have more experience in this area than he does. His inexperience might cause him to think that X is an absolute necessity and the most fabulous idea ever. If your response is in the vein of "Whatever you do, NEVER DO X because it's a terrible idea," then the client could take it as an insult and eliminate you from consideration.

C. Keep all comments short and relatively generic. You never have all of the information you need from the job posting alone, and at least one conversation with the client is always required to execute the task correctly. Don't give the client an excuse to dock you on your feedback later. "Well, in her application, she told me to do A, but after she got the job, she said B was the right response. I don't think she knows what she's talking about." That's a review you never want to get.

3. **What challenging part of this job are you most experienced in?** You should have already answered this with a good cover letter by listing your relevant experience. This question is included because many freelancers don't follow the template above and do a poor job of pitching their skills. Either they haven't included information about their experience or have included such a long cover letter that the client got tired of trying to find the info he needed and just gave up.

Follow the template I gave you and include your relevant experience in your cover letter. In the response box to this question, say something along the lines of: "As I mentioned in my cover letter, I have quite a bit of experience with X." Here, "X" should include the general skill (e.g., graphic design, transcription, or copywriting) and not the specific background (e.g., "One client I had hired me to do this extremely specific task which I already described above"). Keep your answer to a single sentence and refer back to your cover letter.

4. **What part of this project most appeals to you?** Avoid a tremendous amount of detail here. When you ask a generic question, you're going to get a generic response. If you're too

specific, you're creating a risk where there is none. The client could read your answer and think, "But that's not what the job is about. She must be a poor choice for what I need." It's likely that the problem is a poorly-written, generic job description, and not that you didn't understand the task at hand. You could respond by talking about how you love taking ownership of responsibility and making it your own, but the whole time the client is picturing you executing a limited set of duties where she controls every aspect.

Don't introduce risk by trying to compensate for a client's lack of effort. A generic question means a one-sentence response that points the client back to your cover letter. As always, keep answers optimistic and positive.

5. ***What past project or job have you had that is most like this one and why?*** This is another example of a question that a well-structured cover letter would have already answered. Keep responses optimistic, positive, and short, then refer the client back to your cover letter.

6. ***What questions do you have about the project?*** Similar to the first question in this list, if you have a question, ask it. If you don't, then there's no need to come up with one. I've found that it's generally sufficient to say something along the lines of, "Not at this point, but once the job begins, I'll want to know about X." Keep your responses optimistic, positive, and short.

7. ***Which of the required job skills do you feel you are strongest at?*** This question is similar to #3, and your answer should follow the same direction. Believe it or not, I've seen inexperienced clients select both 3 and 7 for the same ad. Keep responses optimistic, positive, short, and point the client back to your cover letter.

8. **Which part of this project do you think will take the most time?** You do not have the information you need to answer this question intelligently. It could be a complicated research project with a relatively simple deliverable, such as an Excel spreadsheet with a list of URLs. Little do you know that this particular client is going to have an extremely specific vision about the Excel format that he can't articulate, and you'll spend hours going back and forth trying to get it right. Don't give him an excuse to say you overbilled him because you locked yourself in with an answer on the application.

   A completely acceptable answer refers to your experience. "In previous, similar projects, I found that the research phase tended to take the most time." Whatever you do, <u>do not</u> answer the question about "this project."

9. **Why did you apply to this particular job?** "Because I think I could do the job and make some money" is a universally applicable, brutally honest answer, but it's not one you should use. Avoid negative responses, such as "I really need the work." You don't want to come across as desperate. An ideal freelancer is self-sufficient enough to pick and choose her projects, and she specifically selected this one out of all of the tasks in the world because she, alone, could knock it out of the park.

   Keep your responses positive, optimistic, and short, then refer the client back to your cover letter. For example, "I really enjoy the X aspect of this kind of work. As you'll see in my cover letter, I've had quite a few jobs like this."

10. **Why do you think you are a good fit for this particular project?** Again, a good cover letter will answer this in spades. Keep responses optimistic, positive, and short, then refer the client back to your cover letter.

You can't leave screening questions blank, you don't want to put all of your eggs in one basket, and you shouldn't duplicate information between the cover letter and screening question responses. Knock the cover letter out of the park, then keep all answers short and sweet and pointed back to your cover letter. The one exception is a customized screening question; remember, if clients ask something specific, it's very important to them and deserves a personalized, detailed response.

Handling Interview Invitations

There are technically two ways to get an "interview" on the Upwork platform, although only one truly counts. When a client posts a job, he can scroll through pages of recommended freelancers and invite them to interview. If you receive an invitation and submit a proposal, you go straight to the top of the list and are automatically considered to be in "Interview" status. You'll see a chat room pop up in your message feed that includes your proposal and attachments.

Do not message the client. He or she has already gotten a message notification, they've seen your proposal, and if they choose not to message you, it means they're not interested. If you have anything to say in a message, you should have included it in your cover letter, and messaging the client with additional information will come off as needy and obnoxious. Although you're in interview "status," you're not being interviewed until the client starts talking to you, which is why this kind doesn't count.

Think of it this way. A client has invited you to apply for a job. You show up to the interview room, and it's empty. You have two choices: you can wait for him to show up, or you can google his address, go to his home, knock on the door, and ask if he'd like to hire you. One of those options is professional, and the other is creepy. Wait for the client.

Keeping Everything on Upwork

Once the client contacts you, however, it's game on. Most of my interviews are conducted via the Upwork messaging system and never involve so much as a phone call; in fact, I've got long-term clients I've collaborated with for over a year and have no idea what their voice sounds like. Upwork also offers video and VOIP (i.e., telephone) conferencing capabilities within the message room itself, so you never have to go outside of the platform to interact with a client.

In fact, you <u>shouldn't</u> go outside of the platform to interview. Upwork recently adjusted its terms of service to require all interviews to be conducted using the communication capabilities they provide: no phone calls, no Zoom or Skype, and no emailing. There is, of course, some flexibility if a client needs your Gmail address to give you access to a Google Drive attachment for the interview, but other than limited exceptions like this, don't go off-platform.

Upwork did this because it discovered a number of freelancers were finding work, interviewing, and then asking the client if they could move off the Upwork site. This prevented Upwork from collecting any commission on the work performed, and they were losing a not-insignificant amount of money. They want to be able to monitor initial communications before the contract is awarded so they can ensure that clients and freelancers alike are abiding by the terms and conditions they agreed to.

This is also good for you. Upwork offers mediation and a certain level of payment guarantees, and staying on the platform means you enjoy access to those services. Depending on the circumstances, Upwork can guarantee payment even if things go bad, and the client refuses to settle up. For fixed-price contracts, Upwork requires that money be deposited in escrow with them before any milestone can go live. The site also offers something called Upwork Payment Protection for any time logged on their hourly app. The site records mouse activity, number of keystrokes, and takes screenshots periodically. If there's a dispute, a site rep can review the logs and confirm that work was actually being done--at worst, Upwork will pay you directly and then pursue reimbursement from the client.

Even if a client prefers a non-Upwork method of communication, I've found that they'll generally respect a gentle reminder that you have to stay on-platform until a contract is awarded. If a client insists on violating this, it's an excellent sign that you don't want this person as a client. Being willing to breach Upwork's terms and conditions is a clear indicator that they'll be willing to void any promises they make to you.

PRO TIP

What happens when Upwork methods don't work? Occasionally you'll run into this situation. More often than not, it isn't the software that's messing up--it's a client who doesn't know how to turn his microphone or speakers on. In that case, try an Upwork-approved method, identify why it didn't work in the chat, then exchange phone numbers and go old school.

Once you get an interview, you're 90 percent of the way there. You've found a job that is a good fit, you've impressed the client with your cover letter and work samples, and she's selected you from among the applicants. The first thing to do is gather a little intel so you go into the interview fully prepared.

Pre-Interview Prep

Revisit the original job posting, where you can see how many freelancers the client is interviewing. If there's only one, that's you, and that's an extremely good sign. You have a much stronger bargaining position if pay becomes a point of negotiation because she's already decided you're who she wants. If she's conducting five interviews, you might have to be a little more flexible if she asks if you're willing to go lower on price--you're up against four other applicants at this point, so you need to ask yourself how low you're ready to go *before you begin the interview*.

If the client wants to chat via video or phone, always confirm what time zone you're referring to when you agree to an appointment. The client's time and time zone are automatically listed next to their name in the chat room; since Upwork is a global platform, it isn't uncommon to have a substantial difference.

Before the interview, try to find the client on the internet. Check out their website, LinkedIn account, and read their bio or company's About Us section, if at all possible. I've won several contracts because it was clear that I had a sense of who they were and could tailor my responses accordingly.

The more homework you can do, the better you're positioning yourself for success. The last thing you want to have happen is to get all the way through the process and end up in second place when only the winner gets paid. It's worth a bit of extra effort at this point, and that often pays off.

In a recent contract, the client wanted to prepare a business proposal and mentioned having to get the approval of a county commissioner for a specific part of Florida. I noticed that he was interviewing four others, and I had to find a way to stand out. I took ten minutes and did a bit of research: I found the county he was from based on some context clues he provided, then the five county commissioners, and then figured out which one he was likely talking about. I looked up that commissioner's bio; when I interviewed the client, I mentioned the commissioner by name and then recommended that he pitch the business proposal in a certain way based on the gentleman's degree and business experience. I was awarded a $700 contract on the spot, and all it took to set me apart was ten minutes of effort.

Conducting the Interview

On the day of the interview, wear a nice shirt. You might be in gym shorts or pajama pants, but if the client pivots and wants to change from a telephone call to a video interview, you don't want your clothing to look like you just had a fight with spaghetti in a blender and lost. Also, take the time to open your webcam and look at your background. You're giving a potential client a peek into your home, and you want the environment to be clean and professional.

Whenever I participate in an interview, I always open up four things: the message room, my proposal, the original job ad, and a blank Word document. The Word doc should already be titled and saved somewhere so you don't risk losing the information. You also don't want to interrupt the interview flow to find a particular folder location and save it in the middle of discussions with the client. If there's the possibility of screen sharing, close all other windows on your computer before beginning.

Spend the ten minutes before the interview reviewing the details of the job they posted and your proposal. Clients are not only interviewing others for the same position, they frequently have multiple ads up, and honest confusion about which job they're interviewing you for can sometimes result. Having everything fresh on your mind will help keep the interview clear of confusion and progressing smoothly.

In the interview, be explicitly clear regarding (1) the work that's being agreed upon, (2) the due dates, and (3) the payment amount and method. The time to handle this is during the interview and negotiation process. Pay particular attention to the financial amounts.

Clients can enter any numbers they want on the job posting, and it isn't uncommon for this to be different than what they're willing to pay. Sometimes this is due to innocent fat-fingering the amounts when they created the post, but occasionally, you'll run across a client who intentionally advertises the job at a high pay rate, then tries to pay you less. If you get the sense that a client has done this deliberately, do not accept the job. I've been fortunate enough not to encounter many of these, but I've engaged with a half dozen or so, and--without exception--they've been nightmares.

Once you've nailed the interview, the client will send over a job offer. Before you accept, take a moment to review the details and confirm that they're what you agreed to. When a client clicks the button to hire you, the offer defaults to information they'd put into the job advertisement, which might be different from what was discussed later. Due dates, in particular, are critical. A busy client can hire you with an auto-populated due date; a few days later, he's reviewing the dozen contracts he has open with various freelancers and notices you "missed" a deadline. It's an honest misunderstanding, but taking a moment to confirm the details before accepting the offer keeps everyone on the same page.

Declined Bids

Although most of the time, clients will simply ignore all of the bids from freelancers they don't hire, sometimes your proposal will get officially declined. If that happens, you'll get an email with a reason why. These are pre-scripted reasons, so don't take them personally.

I know from personal experience that it can be discouraging to get these notifications, but don't let it get to you. Learn what you can from it, forget it, and move on.

Upwork

Here are some similar jobs that are available

Hi Joshua,

Your proposal for experienced native English copy writer needed for website and presentations was declined for the following reason: Just preferred other applicants

There are a lot of jobs that require your skills. Consider submitting a proposal for one of the following:

Bidding Strategies

Bidding should be intentional, and how you approach it will vary depending on how much work you have and how much you need. These are the top four strategies I use, in descending order of how frequently I employ them.

Maintenance Bidding. Once you have a full plate of work, regardless of whether that's two hours a week or fifty, start bidding on your next round of contracts. Because you're not desperate for work, you have a stronger bargaining position and can be more selective in which contracts you pursue. When I'm in this stage, my goal is to bid on one to two high-value contracts every day. Doing this consistently allows you to maximize and maintain your pay rate.

Bidding Frenzy. One approach is to blitz the ads over a short period. When I'm doing this, I'll stay logged into Upwork and check my job feed and saved searches every hour, then bid for every job that interests me. Consolidating your bids during this time typically results in a higher contract win rate, and I can usually get 2-3 week's worth of work within three days, then I don't have to worry about anything other than maintenance bidding.

Client Pinging. Reaching out to former clients and asking if they have any work available can sometimes yield fruit. If so, it's a win from several perspectives. Repeat contracts with the same client positively impact your JSS, and you're presumably working with someone you liked in the first place. The downside of this approach is that it doesn't have a high success rate. You're generally reaching out to someone who is comfortable using Upwork as a client; if they don't have an open ad, they likely don't have work. That isn't always the case, though, so it's worth a shot.

Wagering Work. This is a bit of a gray area here. While Upwork's terms and conditions don't allow free sample tasks to be performed, they don't have any problem with not charging clients for work that doesn't meet their satisfaction. The way to satisfy both Upwork and the client is to quote what the work would be, then tell them that if it meets their expectations, they'll pay for it; if the work doesn't measure up, they don't pay for it. You'll start a contract, the client will deposit the funds into escrow, and you'll knock out the task. Only do this if you're confident you can knock it out of the park.

Ten-Dollar Ladder. This is a strategy I used heavily during the first eight months of my freelancing career. I was trying to figure out at what level the market would value my work. I started at $25 an hour and bid until I had a full plate of work. I'd immediately raise my rates by $10 an hour and begin bidding for the next batch. Once I had a full plate at $35 an hour, I did the same with $45, then continued that process until I landed at an equilibrium. I also use this approach when I'm developing a new skill set and want to see how the market values it.

High & Hold. When you have as much work as you can handle, raise your profile rates by an absurd amount; I typically bump it up by $40 an hour. This does two things: first, it discourages getting a high number of invitations you have to deal with (if you ignore them, you can get dinged on Upwork), and you don't have time to monitor invitations continually when you're this busy. Second, if you do get invited at this rate, bid it--you might win. If you do, you just got a $40/hour pay bump. I've had this happen a couple of times. It isn't often, but it's frequent enough to be effective.

Managing Non-Traditional Job Offers

A relatively rare scenario is being sent a contract offer out of the blue. A client can create an invite-only job that isn't publicly posted, pick your profile out, and then send a contract offer without you having any idea what's going on. This has happened to me four times, with mixed results. Two of the clients ended up being good, and I was very glad I turned down the other two. If this happens to you, don't accept the offer before you've talked over the details with the potential client; once you agree to a job, it begins to impact your Upwork feedback, which is your lifeblood. An unsolicited lucrative offer in your inbox could be a winning lottery ticket or an email offer from a Nigerian prince that involves Western Union.

I advertise that I'm a professional freelance writer on my LinkedIn profile, and I've had several clients find me and offer work via that social network. If that contact occurred off Upwork, you're not required to bring the client onto the platform, but it's a good idea. Upwork has an option called "Direct Contracts," where you bring a client onto the platform after you both have already agreed to work with each other. When you bring a client with you, Upwork's fees drop to 3.4 percent; in return, they handle payment details and any dispute issues. Those services are worth it to me to avoid any potential headache with a client who might decide to be difficult. In this case, you create the contract and send it to a non-Upwork client, so they don't even have to create an account.

Summary

Bidding well is a cornerstone of being a competitive freelancer. Because it's related to salesmanship and bragging about yourself, it's a skill many of us aren't naturally comfortable with. If this is you, understand that you're not alone--but also realize that this is something you must learn to do well, or you won't make it.

Be intentional about bidding. If you notice something that is working, keep it. If you're not getting any bites, go back to the basics and don't be afraid to revamp everything. Take a critical look at where things are breaking down. If you're not getting discovered (you can find this in your "My Stats" section), then you may not be classifying your skills correctly on your profile. If you're getting looked at, but not interviewed, your title, overview, and profile portfolio might need to be revamped. If you're getting interviewed but not hired, then work on your interview skills. Ask yourself whether you're driving too hard of a bargain, if you're pressing too hard, or if you're coming across as desperate. Do potential clients perceive you as obnoxious or challenging to work with? Being very honest with yourself is the only way you'll improve.

Chapter Five Exercise

Start a spreadsheet tracker in Excel or Google Sheets. List all of the bids you've placed and their eventual result. Note which ones you didn't get hired on and where the process broke down. (Remember to check these ads and disregard any where the job was canceled and no one was hired--that's a client issue, not a freelancer problem.) If you notice a trend, identify where that problem is likely occurring, then rework that section of your approach.

Date of Bid	Job Title	Experience Level	Hourly Fixed Price Retainer	Hourly Bid Range	Hourly Bid Rate	Fixed Price Budget	Fixed Price Bid	Proposal Declined?	Interviewed?	Hired?
14 Aug 2020	resume builder (experienced in Federal IT and leadership)	Expert	Fixed Price	N/A	N/A	$130	$300	No	Yes	Yes
14 Aug 2020	Needed: YouTube script writer on weekly basis	Intermediate	Fixed Price	N/A	N/A	$100	$240	No	No	No
14 Aug 2020	Write 45-50 Multiple Choice Questions for Literacy Program	Intermediate	Fixed Price	N/A	N/A	$200	$250	No	Yes	Yes
12 Aug 2020	Privacy law writer	Expert	ly Fixed Price Ret	$25 - $50	$85	N/A	N/A	No	No	No

CHAPTER SIX

Executing a Contract Successfully

Once you've been awarded a contract, it's time to execute. More than your immediate paycheck is at stake here: Upwork is a feedback-intensive platform, so investing in your reputation with positive client relationship management is crucial. In this chapter, I'll cover the most vital elements of interacting with clients. Some of these are universal, and you can apply them wherever you freelance, while others are more specific to Upwork itself.

Clarifying Expectations

This seems like it should be common sense. Still, it's essential to establish a foundation of professionalism while freelancing in an almost exclusively virtual environment. You've likely seen how easy it is for messages to get twisted around over email or text; with Upwork, you're going to be conducting 90 percent of business without ever speaking or video chatting with your client.

In Chapter Five, I discussed the importance of nailing down work details before accepting a contract offer. The first contract I had that went south was with a fellow who wanted to write a story about how he'd had some negative interactions with a few police officers.

They'd known each other since high school, there was some bad blood, which eventually developed into a bad experience in a professional capacity. My client had already won a six-figure civil suit against the city, so I figured that the story was legitimate and would be relatively easy to tell. We hammered out the details of the contract: price, deadlines, length, and deliverables. It was a fixed-price contract; he funded the first milestone, then sent me the first batch of documents.

I thought I had done a good job of nailing everything down, but it quickly fell apart. The client sent me reams of information and then clarified his expectation that I pour over every document and videotaped interview from court proceedings that had lasted for more than a year and a half. I asked him simply to tell me his story, and then I could write it and reference the appropriate documents. He refused. It turns out that we had a simple miscommunication that altered the entire project: when he hired me to tell his story, I assumed that he would tell me what happened in his own words, and then I'd turn it into a polished product. He expected just to give me thousands of pages of documents, hundreds of hours of video interviews, and then figure out the story on my own… for $600.

We reached an impasse: I told him that I couldn't dedicate most of the next year to digging into his story without switching to an hourly contract, and he refused to tell me his story or budge on price. I ended up having to cancel the contract, but I learned two lessons. First, even the simplest assumptions can create massive headaches, so clarifying expectations upfront is crucial. Second, my Upwork reputation was saved because I didn't accept a dollar from him. A canceled contract doesn't show up on your profile, meaning the client can't rate or review you. However, the moment he pays you anything, he can. I'd already dedicated five hours to the project, but I chose to absorb that cost rather than attempt to force him to pay through an

Upwork dispute. Sometimes professionalism involves taking the high road and eating expenses to focus on what's more important: your reputation.

Putting the Client's Satisfaction First

In another contract, I served as the editor in chief for a news site and hired numerous freelancers to work for me. I hired a young writer and sent her a two-page welcome letter I'd created for all freelancers on the team. In it, I clarified subject material, formatting instructions, and length requirements.

The freelancer submitted her first article, and it was immediately apparent that she hadn't read the first word of the welcome PDF. Nothing was on target. I returned it to her with a summary of what was wrong, but she refused to correct anything until she had been paid for her initial efforts. Her refusal to work with me eliminated any gray area where I would have given her the benefit of the doubt. Based on her stubborn attitude, I ended the contract that would have been long-term and lucrative for her.

Seeing this from the client perspective was eye-opening; although this was a very black and white example, I took it to heart. From that point forward, I made my clients a guarantee: with any fixed-price contract, I would edit the product as often as needed to guarantee satisfaction. As long as no new requirements were introduced, their satisfaction was my top priority.

There have been a few times where there was quite a bit more back and forth than I would have liked, and I felt that it was due to the client's failure to communicate their requirements clearly. However, far more often than not, when a client knows that you're committed to their satisfaction, they open the deliverable with an optimistic mindset and rarely request significant revisions. I seldom have to work beyond a second draft, which starts with my willingness to send as many drafts as necessary.

Taking the Blame

I pride myself on rarely getting a deliverable wrong. Occasionally, however, a client and I completely miss each other in translation. I once had a client hire me to write a paper worth $200. I sent her the first draft, and she responded that I had completely missed the boat. I got further clarification from her, completely rewrote it, and she gave me the same feedback for round two.

She called me and said she'd ended up writing it herself. She knew that I'd spent a substantial amount of time working on it, and she wanted to pay me something for my efforts, but the frustration in her voice clearly communicated she didn't want to pay full price. I told her my policy: if a client isn't happy with the work, she doesn't pay for it--period. The frustration turned to surprise and almost shock. I didn't charge her a penny, because I only wanted to be paid if I'd earned it.

Within three hours, I had a long-term contract offer from her for a different type of writing that was much more clearly defined, and it ended up being worth $3,400. To this day, I still haven't found out what she wanted out of that original paper, but taking the blame for the miscommunication ended up making me 17 times more than what I would have had I insisted on arguing with her and insisting on payment. Sometimes a bit of humility goes a long way.

Honesty is Always the Best Policy

I once had a long-term project management contract with a large Fortune 500 company. I hired quite a few freelancers in this role and oversaw every aspect of their performance, including payment and feedback. The contracts required that I hire freelancers with similar skillsets in batches, and it was always fascinating to me when I compared work diaries between the contractors. They were being required to do identical work, and some variance was expected based on their individual work speed. When someone artificially inflated their hours, however, it stood out like a sore thumb.

I'm not talking about a ten percent variation here--some freelancers would bill four or five times the amount of hours that everyone else on their team did. I'd let them go and put them on a "Do Not Rehire" list, and they'd never work for that corporation again. I always shook my head when that happened. The company loved rehiring good workers and never hesitated to pay full rates. The work was relatively easy, and I saw freelancers earn thousands of dollars on contract after contract. The people who put short-term gain before honesty, however? We'd let them go with the couple hundred dollars they'd earned, and that was it.

Although honesty is always the best policy, it needs to be communicated professionally. I remember looking at a freelancer's feedback and reviews one time when I discovered a very detailed response left by a client. The freelancer had just been fired from a virtual assistant position because she consistently used her children as an excuse to avoid agreed-upon job tasks. The client quoted statements from her consisting of things like, "Sorry, my kid just vomited all over my keyboard, so…" This was one of several examples. The client had listed these in her public feedback as a warning to other clients of the type of freelancer they were considering. Stuff happens, and we all get that. Just handle it appropriately and professionally on your own, and everything will work out. Beyond those caveats, however, being very straightforward and upfront will take you far as an independent contractor.

Developing the Right Mindset

Most of the time, what a client needs and what she wants are in alignment. Occasionally, however, they conflict with each other, and you need to be clear on how to handle that before the situation happens.

I once had a client hire me to rewrite her LinkedIn profile. We discussed what she wanted to achieve. I felt that I had a pretty clear grasp on her desired result: she wanted to communicate her style (which was bubbly, vivacious, and enthusiastic) in a LinkedIn format. I drafted the summary and emailed it to her. She wasn't happy with the product. It turns out she wanted things like far more words in all caps and lots of exclamation points. I tried to explain to her how that was outside of LinkedIn communication norms. Even such high-profile motivational speakers as Tony Robbins and Les Brown didn't have LinkedIn profiles that were written in that way.

She would have none of it and refused my request to give it a second shot. My pride was hurt, and I spent a few days blaming her in my mind. "How dare she question my expertise," I thought. "She hired me because I know what I'm doing, but when I gave her what she needed, she insulted the quality of my work."

As I thought about it, though, I realized that hiring me for my expertise was only part of what made a contract. I owed her an educated, informed answer on her questions. I did the right thing by explaining to her what LinkedIn norms were and what her profile should consist of. Where I went wrong, however, was giving her something she didn't want. At the end of the day, that's what's most important. She might have reasons for structuring it that way that I don't know about. What matters is delivering what she wanted, and if I couldn't do that, I shouldn't accept the contract. The client's expectations define success.

When Things Go Well

There are four aspects to a contract:

1. What the client wants
2. The deadline
3. What the client gets
4. The feedback

In Chapter Five, I talked about getting on the same page with clients regarding precisely what they want before agreeing to the contract, so that takes care of #1. When it comes to the other three, there's one principle to keep in mind above all else: always under-promise and over-deliver. It can be tempting to promise the sky, the clouds, and the birds that fly in it to get the contract, particularly if you're in a bad spot. However, it's critical to remember that the most important aspect of freelancing is your reputation--period. The most crucial element of building and maintaining a good reputation is expectation management.

Handling timelines. When you're setting deadlines with a client, pick the date you think is realistic, then add two business days to it. If a client needs it 48 hours earlier, he'll let you know. In other words, if you're up against a hard timeline, you'll know about it. For the vast majority of projects, however, the client just wants to know when he can expect the work to be completed. People don't mentally track deliverables in terms of time; they think about them in terms of "early," "on-time," or "late." Over the life of a contract, you're going to develop a reputation as routinely fitting into one of those three categories. Make sure it's the first or second, but never the third.

Giving yourself that cushion also provides flexibility if unexpected, quick-turn work comes in from other clients. Two days before I wrote this portion of the book, a former client called me with a rush order that had to be done in a matter of hours. I was on track for all of my deadlines, so I shuffled around a couple of projects and picked up a paycheck I wouldn't have been able to if I'd been stretched for time. Since you can charge a premium for emergency orders, you're creating a constant availability to pick up the most lucrative work available to you.

Finally, structuring your calendar this way decreases stress. One of the aspects of freelancing I've most enjoyed is how much pressure has dissipated from my life. I've realized that I can get the same amount and type of work done on a firefighting basis or an easy-chair basis. In the former, I'm not proactively managing client expectations. Every day feels like I'm coming from behind, prioritizing the biggest emergencies rather than what I should be doing at the moment. With the latter approach, I just casually take care of whatever needs to be done that day, then live life. Nothing is different about the tasks I'm executing--it's 100 percent expectation management.

One quick note about receiving good feedback: when clients leave feedback on your profile, you can respond with a single comment. This feature is designed to allow you to provide further context if someone leaves you good feedback, but it's also available when you get a five-star rating. If it's a good review, leave it alone. I've seen a couple of freelancer profiles where they responded with an enthusiastic "Thank You!" to each good rating, and it comes off as needy and desperate. If you get a good review, feel free to shoot them a private note expressing your gratitude (in fact, I'd encourage it), but don't respond publicly. I remember a line from an old radio show where one of the main characters told another: "You're the only person I know who can ruin gratitude by expressing it." Don't be that person.

How to be Successful with Fixed-Price Work

There are two basic kinds of payment models: fixed-price and hourly work. With the first, you're paid on a per-task or per-item basis. If you complete the job more quickly than you had anticipated, then your day becomes more profitable. If it takes longer than you expected, you have to eat the cost. When you're first starting, you probably won't have any idea how long it takes you to knock out most tasks. Building up that data will be crucial to ensuring profitability on fixed-price jobs.

When you get a new contract, pull up an Excel spreadsheet and describe the task. Time how long it takes you to execute the first draft, then do the same if you need to make any corrections. List how much you were paid, and maintain that spreadsheet as you move through subsequent contracts. You'll begin to dial in how long each task takes. All that remains at that point is determining how much you want to make per hour; if you want to make $40 per hour and a particular type of task takes 1.5 hours, you'll need to charge $60 for it. I can write an average of 600 words an hour (including research and reference time) on a topic I'm not familiar with. I want to bill $85 an hour, so I know that I need to charge 14 cents a word for fixed-price jobs.

As you bid on different kinds of work, your spreadsheet will continue to grow with your skills. You'll also notice that your speed and the quality of your work increases, making each day more profitable. On the other side of the coin, you'll discover what kind of work you *don't* want to do. When I began freelancing, I had no idea what kind of writing was even available, let alone what I would be good at. I started with resumes, because that's what I knew I could execute well, and then branched out into other styles as those opportunities became available. I'll pick up a resume job from time to time, but I've had exposure to so much at this point that I've realized resumes are one of my least favorite types of work, so I tend to bid on everything else first.

Fixed-price jobs are based on client-created milestones. A milestone contains a description of a specific product, and a client has to fund the milestone by surrendering those funds to Upwork, which holds them in escrow. Before beginning work on a task, ask your client to fund a milestone for it. If you don't, then you're removing Upwork's ability to mediate any billing disputes that might arise; if things go south with the client, you might be surrendering that work for free. Although this rarely happens, if you freelance for long enough, you'll end up in a billing dispute. It's best to operate consistently each time, so when this does happen, you're prepared for it.

Hourly contracts are different in several ways. If a job consists of a single task, it's more likely to be fixed-price. If you're being hired to knock out a variety of functions, you're much more likely to be paid by the hour because it's simpler for the client. I've found that long-term work is slightly more geared toward hourly billing, so if you've got a client who will keep you around for a year, you're a bit more likely to be paid by the hour.

Approaching Hourly Work Correctly

There are two ways you can bill hourly labor on the Upwork platform. The first (and default) method is to use their hourly tracker. It's a small software application that you start when you begin working on a particular contract; it tracks the number of keystrokes and amount of mouse activity, then periodically takes screenshots of what you're doing. There are pros and cons to this approach. On the plus side, it's convenient, and you don't have to pay strict attention to the clock since the app does it for you. The flip side is that it can cause a bit of anxiety in some folks because clients and Upwork staff have a very incisive look at what you're doing. Casually corresponding with other clients while you work, for example, or briefly pulling up your bank website to pay a bill can make it look like you're not putting your full effort into what a client is paying you to do.

The other method of billing hourly work is manual. If you prefer this method, you'll have to explicitly ask your client to enable it, since it's disabled by default. Billing disputes are much easier for Upwork to investigate and handle when they have the forensic evidence provided by the tracker, so they prefer that you use the app.

If you do end up tracking and billing hours manually, you need to ensure that you're billing accurately. Track your start and stop times on each project and stay focused. It can be tempting to fudge your hours a bit, but stay away from this at all costs. Beyond integrity, there are two logistical reasons for it. I've mentioned previously that freelancing in general and Upwork specifically is heavily based on reputation. Your profile and cover letter become your resume and reference sheet. If you're consistently dinged, even to a small degree, it adds up over time and negatively impacts your ability to get new work.

You can adjust your work diary after the fact, even if it's recorded with the hourly tracker, but it needs to be during the billing week. There are several reasons to do this. I once realized that I'd selected the wrong contract and billed four hours of work to the wrong client, so I had to go in and delete those hours and manually add them to the correct contract. Another time, I was working for a client whose website started with "fac." I began to typo it into my browser and hit enter as it auto-populated, only to watch in horror as it opened Facebook just as the tracker snapped a screenshot. I was able to delete the screenshot, which also deleted about ten minutes' worth of billable time. Still, it was worth it to avoid having my meme addiction officially documented with a client.

If you forget that your hourly tracker is on and walk away from your computer, it will remain active, but won't bill the client further after you've been idle for ten minutes. This is good, but it's also something to be aware of. I've occasionally had contracts where I had to watch video or listen to audio for significant periods; my tracker was happily snapping away at the bottom of the window, but since I didn't use my mouse or keyboard during that time, it wasn't billed. Just be sure to click or hit a key every ten minutes or so if you're working a task like this.

When Things Go Badly

In previous sections, I've outlined how to prevent things from going downhill in various stages. Here, we'll focus on what happens after you've been awarded a contract, submitted work, and client relations deteriorate.

Things can go sideways for many reasons. If you're honest, clarify deliverables and due dates before accepting a contract offer, and accurately represent the quality of work you can deliver, the only things you're leaving to chance are how the client handles himself or herself. I've had over 100 contracts over the last two and a half years, and 85 percent of them have been flawless: excellent clients, clear communication, and quick payment. I've had some level of trouble with about 15 percent. Clients are no different than freelancers: they're all people, and there are good ones, bad ones, and then a fair number who just aren't a good fit.

Unclear expectations. Of the contracts that had issues, most were relatively low-key, and I parted ways with the client amicably. One recurring theme I've encountered involves clients with unclear expectations, and the most common cause of that was them not knowing what they wanted. This led to them either being dissatisfied with the products I provided or wanting me to keep working for free until they figured out what they wanted. Sometimes clients are blind to how much work they're asking you to do. I had one client who started the contract shotgunning me everything that made him think of me, including YouTube videos he wanted me to watch and even a clip of his favorite jazz band. Because these were interspersed with work materials, I didn't know what was what and watched them all--on billed time. He was surprised when he got the hourly invoice, but when I explained where the time was going, the extra emails dried up quickly. In these cases, a calm, honest conversation usually clarifies the issue or determines that we aren't a good fit for each other. You can typically end the contract without any problems.

Nightmare clients. Occasionally you run into genuinely horrible people. The most frequent problem I've encountered here involves clients who agree to a set rate of pay then consistently try to negotiate it down *after* the contract has been awarded. In one case, a client advertised a job for $500, agreed to $300, asked me to perform the first task as a test for $100, and then after approving me for subsequent work, wanted to pay me $50 for the same product. In these cases, following the guidelines I've outlined above kept me from surrendering free work or ever being paid less than I'd agreed to.

Handling subpar feedback. I'll give you two examples of how handling sub-five-star feedback can go either way. I hired a freelancer once who significantly underperformed. When the contract ended, I gave her 4.5 stars, and she immediately came back with a vengeance. Her initial message demanded that I explain why I'd given her "such bad feedback." I outlined the specific areas where she'd fallen short and why I'd marked her down. She continued to come back in a manner that I can't describe as anything short of vicious, but I noticed a consistent theme in what she was saying. Not once did she address her performance; the entire message she was communicating was how my feedback was the problem.

I learned from that experience. When a client left me a 4.2-star feedback a few months later, I messaged him and asked what I could have done differently to earn five stars. He explained that I'd made a formatting mistake on my first draft; even though I'd corrected it on the second and final draft, he'd marked me down slightly. I thanked him for the feedback and didn't fight him on it.

Apparently, he couldn't get my question out of his head. The next day he messaged me. He wanted to know why I cared about what was, to him, such a minor markdown. I explained how valuable feedback was on the Upwork platform, that I always wanted to earn five stars, and I needed to learn from any experience where I delivered less than stellar work. He immediately responded that he didn't realize it had such a significant impact and asked me to reopen the feedback so he could adjust it. I did so, and when I checked back in an hour, he'd upped it to five stars.

Treating people respectfully goes a long way. When you show that you value their opinion, are humble, and want to learn from the experience, you'd be surprised how eager most clients are to give you great feedback.

Working Through a Dispute

Disputes typically revolve around a freelancer submitting work and a client refusing to pay because it doesn't meet standards. I've been involved with a dispute from each perspective.

As a client, I once commissioned a video and hired a video editor. I gave him specific instructions about the clips I wanted him to use, the text and footage that should accompany it, and the order in which it should progress. Over the course of a half dozen revisions, he repeatedly failed to do the things I'd asked of him, so I fired him, hired someone else, and only gave him partial payment. He initiated a dispute, Upwork looked into it, and the platform sided with me.

As a freelancer, I had a client subcontract a portion of a website redesign project to me. We agreed on the product, deadline, and price, and I wrote and submitted the work. When he received it, he was delighted with the product but requested that I add a new section that nearly doubled the original article's length. I was billing him on a per-word basis, and he'd funded the milestone for the original commission, but when I charged him for the additional work, he confessed he didn't have the means to pay. I finally had to accept a partial payment because the money to cover the extra work wasn't in escrow.

The dispute process. Upwork has separate procedures for disputing hourly and fixed-price work. Hourly disputes tend to be initiated by the client. Since the freelancer submits his or her hours to Upwork and Upwork charges the client's card, payment is typically painless. The only time when this wouldn't be the case is if the client's card has been maxed or canceled during the workweek, and Upwork can't access the funds. In this case, the Upwork Payment Protection program guarantees payment as long as you've been using their app--even if Upwork has to pay you themselves. Manual hours do not qualify for this protection, so I typically only bill manual hours for established clients with excellent payment history.

Hourly disputes. For a client to dispute a freelancer's hours, she must initiate the process within five business days after the billing period ends. Upwork debits the billed amount from the client's payment method, then freezes the funds while a dispute specialist looks into it. Once the specialist's investigation is complete, he decides who gets the funds. If the client has used the tracker and the record clearly shows he was working on the client's project during all billed hours, he wins. If the log shows something else, or if he billed manual hours, then the client will most likely win the dispute.

Fixed-price disputes. More commonly, freelancers initiate disputes over fixed-price contracts after work has been submitted and payment hasn't been approved. Three situations are typically responsible for this:

1. A freelancer completes and submits work for which a milestone hasn't been created and funded.
2. A client ends a job while there's still an escrow balance.
3. A client refuses to release a milestone payment after work has been delivered.

In the first case, Upwork's position is that work hasn't been formally commissioned until a milestone has been created and funded, which makes sense. If you submit work before it's been funded, then you don't have a payment guarantee.

In the second case, the client must request a freelancer's agreement for funds to be returned to them. If the freelancer agrees, the money is returned to the client's account immediately. If the freelancer ignores the request, the money is returned to the client in 14 days. If the freelancer disputes the return, an Upwork dispute specialist gets involved and investigates the issue. Responsiveness is critical. The specialist will make two attempts to contact each party; if one side doesn't respond to the second attempt, the other party wins the dispute.

When it comes to the third case, patience is a critical starting point for a freelancer. If you simply send the work to the client, they're under no pressure to pay and can approve the milestone at their leisure.

If you formally request payment by clicking on the "Submit Work for Payment" button, it starts a 14-day countdown. The client has three options: approve the milestone, allow the timeline to expire (in which case, the payment is automatically approved), or request changes to the work, which stops the countdown and puts the ball back in your court. If the client has disappeared or indicated that he doesn't want to pay but hasn't formally requested changes on a funded milestone, you simply need to wait--the funds will be credited to your account in two weeks. When a client requests changes that you can't make or create additional work outside of the scope of your agreement, that's when you can initiate a dispute.

Fixed-price contracts are relatively easy to investigate if you abide by Upwork's processes outlined in this book. Stay on the Upwork platform, so everything is visible to a dispute specialist. Agree to specific terms of work before accepting the contract, including both payment amounts and due dates. Require that the client create and fund a milestone before beginning work. Set realistic timelines for yourself and submit finished products early. If you do that, your chances of winning the dispute are very high. If you skip any of those steps, you begin to compromise your position, and Upwork will likely side with the client.

Preventing formal disputes. Upwork encourages resolving disputes between yourselves whenever possible, and this is nearly always the best option. It's certainly the first step you should attempt. If negotiations break down, then Upwork will step in with dispute resolution services. If those break down, they'll try to mediate between the parties and offer a non-binding recommendation. In cases where that isn't an acceptable resolution, it can proceed to formal arbitration.

This rarely occurs, and it's rarely worth your time to go this far. The only time I would recommend it is if you have a massive amount of money on the line, such as finishing a project and requesting the several thousand dollars you're owed in a lump sum. However, you should never agree to such a payment scheme in the first place. Agree to a series of milestones in manageable amounts; if there's a dispute at any point, it's easier to correct with work revisions or resolve with a dispute specialist, and less money and emotional energy are riding on the outcome.

In two and a half years and approximately 500 contracts as both a freelancer and client, I've only had a dozen payment disagreements, most of which were resolved without ever proceeding to a formal dispute. I've been satisfied with the outcome of both disputes I've had, and I've never personally seen a case proceed to arbitration. I'm sure it happens, but it's exceedingly rare--as it should be with a good process (like Upwork has) and proper execution (like you will if you follow the best practices in this book).

Where Negative Feedback Appears

If you freelance for long enough, you'll end up disagreeing with a client over something that will result in each of you removing the other person from your Christmas card list. Even if payments can be resolved and there's an amicable separation, you might open your ended contract to find an unpleasant review. There are three primary flavors of bad feedback.

Invisible feedback. The first is actually one you can't see. When a contract ends, both of you can submit private feedback to Upwork regarding whether you'd recommend working with the other person again. This impacts your freelancing Job Success Score (JSS), which is visible on your profile and updates every two weeks. You'll find a detailed breakdown and explanation of the JSS in Chapter #. A client can give you five stars and a Nobel Prize-winning public feedback and still mark you down privately, although this is rare. Far more commonly, the private feedback will mirror the public feedback, so you can gauge whether you need to be worried about your JSS or not.

A word of caution: since you can't see this, you may or may not be able to deduce what happened. If you've only closed out one contract in a month and your JSS takes a hit, then you can be pretty sure that client dinged you privately. If you've closed out multiple during that period, you won't be able to tell where the negative feedback came from. I was acting as a project manager for a client one time and had hired several freelancers. At the end of the work cycle, I closed contracts for a half dozen people. A week later, one of the contractors came back and immediately lit into me for being deceptive in my feedback, accusing me of lying and several other things. I checked what I'd given him, and it had been solid on both the public and private fronts. Not only that, but I'd also put him on my rehire list. As you can imagine, I took him off the list and gave him a "no rehire" classification for that organization, eliminating several thousand dollars worth of work he could have had down the line.

What you can see. The second type of feedback consists of star ratings, and this impacts your JSS. Since it's visible, it also affects your ability to procure future work. Upwork is a feedback-intensive platform with a very positive culture, meaning the assumption is that if you fulfill all of the work you agreed to and it's within specs and on-time, you should earn the full five stars. If you see someone who has less than five stars on a contract, the implication is that they failed to deliver in some way.

Optional comments. The third type of feedback is an optional comment. Whether a client leaves a comment or not is irrelevant when it comes to your JSS, but these are crucial when it comes to continued success as a freelancer. When you bid for a job, clients can view your profile and quickly scroll through your closed contracts. If they see a string of positive comments, your odds of getting a job go up. If they see a series of poor comments, they likely won't hire you. If they see a preponderance of no feedback, they'll be leery, and who gets the job might come down to which freelancer seems to be most popular with past clients.

What you should do. When work is complete on a contract and it's about to close, I always ask clients if I've done everything I can to earn five stars. If not, then I ask for the opportunity to fix it for free before the contract closes. Doing this accomplishes several things for you. First, it gives them the chance to tell you if they have anything against you or your work. Second, it creates the subtle implication and social pressure that, if they don't respond, they need to put down five stars.

I've noticed that clients will often give less than the full five stars when freelancers don't do this, even if the freelancer delivered as promised. It's as if the client will go down the list and think, "Well, I wish he (i.e., you) would have communicated a bit more proactively here," or "It would have been nice if he responded within an hour when I messaged," or "I would have liked it if he had gotten me the products a day earlier." This leads to a string of 4.5 to 4.9 ratings on a contractor's profile. While these aren't bad at all, if you're a finalist for contract consideration and you're marked down slightly on every contract while your competition has an unbroken string of five stars, guess who will get the job?

Preventing Negative Feedback

The best way to deal with lousy feedback is to prevent it from happening in the first place. In 90 percent of cases, just delivering quality work on time will be fine, but occasionally you'll have a client who dislikes some aspect of how you operate, even if you fulfilled the contract. In this case, asking for feedback like I outlined above *before* the contract ends goes a long way toward smoothing out that interaction. Clients are less likely to feel like they have to communicate any small dissatisfaction in permanent feedback if you proactively allow them to express that in private message rooms.

It's important to remember that, in this particular case, **the customer is always right**. They might not always be right when it comes to payment--you don't have to accept a lower rate just because they feel like paying you less. They might not be right when it comes to super-human product expectations, and that's fine. But here, you're asking for their opinion; even if you disagree with it, **the customer is always right**. You don't get to tell them their opinion is wrong; the only thing you can do is attempt to reshape it. Do not react if they express dissatisfaction in a particular area. You're creating a vent so they can show any toxicity toward you in messages and not in a way that will impact your freelancing career.

If you can provide details that will give further insight or help explain why you made a call that you did, it might be appropriate to produce those here. However, only include those if it can be done positively. If you feel like what you want to say will be perceived as a disagreement, just clamp your lips shut and take the feedback. Humbly apologize for the miscommunication or misunderstanding, thank them for their honesty, and then offer to make it right.

When clients are irritated by something small, the number one desire they have is just to be listened to and, more importantly, heard. When you ask them the five-star question, you're allowing them to be heard. When you refuse to disagree with them and defend yourself, you're showing that their opinion matters and that they're being listened to. I've had contracts where I feared negative feedback and comments pull a 180 when I made sure the client felt like she could say what she wanted to, and I'd listen.

Ending the contract without payment. Another way to prevent bad feedback is to end the contract before you're paid anything. It's better to lose a hundred dollars now than to deal with poison on your profile. If you close a job before you're paid anything, it counts as a canceled contract and not a poorly-fulfilled one. The client doesn't get the opportunity to leave feedback on your work, and it doesn't impact your JSS as significantly (although it can slightly). Although this isn't a great option, sometimes it's the lesser of the two evils.

I had one contract where a client was explicitly clear on the article she wanted me to write. She gave me an outline with main points in a specific order, six articles from which to pull evidence, and a narrow target for word count. I hit every objective she'd outlined, submitted the work, and she came back and said that what I'd sent her "wasn't at all" what she wanted. I asked for clarification on what she wanted me to change, and she couldn't give me any specifics. At that point, even though I didn't know the reason, I knew she couldn't or wouldn't be satisfied. I closed the contract, accepted it as a life lesson learned, and moved on.

Choosing not to charge. Another policy I personally have is that I never charge for work that isn't up to par, and I've seen what this looks like from both the client and freelancing perspective. I had one contract as the editor in chief for a news site where I oversaw approximately one dozen writers. Whenever I hired a new freelancer, I'd send them a two-page welcome letter with all of the specs for how to get topics approved, structure the article, and format it in WordPress to fit our style. I had a writer once who haphazardly submitted her first article without getting the topic approved, and it didn't meet our style or format requirements. She had completely ignored the elements in the welcome letter. I kicked it back to her with feedback, and she instantly told me that she wanted to get paid for her efforts before she changed anything at all. I paid her a reduced amount, closed the contract, left negative feedback, then moved on. Occasional misunderstandings are inevitable, and I wouldn't have had any issue if she'd acknowledged her mistakes and corrected them. The obstinate refusal to fix her errors without being paid first was an immediate turn-off, and she killed a contract that was worth several thousand dollars.

I've had three instances as a freelancer where a client said that the work I delivered was unacceptable. In each case, I could point to the client's direction and show how it met the specs they gave me; in none of the three could the client specifically articulate why it was wrong. But my policy stood, and I didn't charge them for the work. In the case I mentioned above, the client was belligerent and almost seemed vengeful, so I immediately ended the contract. In the other two cases, the client wasn't so much displeased as just dissatisfied, so I tried to salvage the relationship. I apologized for the miscommunication, told them they didn't owe me a cent and asked if there was anything I could do to make up for it. In both of the other cases, the client was so impressed by that response that they hired me for further work, which proceeded smoothly. I ended up earning nearly $7,000 between those two contracts after having to eat less than $400, so this approach definitely pays off.

Removing Negative Feedback

You can use this to your advantage in several ways. If I have a potentially negative review waiting for my response and I'm about to go into an intense bidding cycle, I leave it. I don't even want to take the chance that whatever is there and the fallout from it could impact my ability to get new work. Even if I can get it removed, I know it will affect my emotions and headspace, and I don't want to deal with that when I'm bidding and need to maximize my confidence--so I ignore it. When that week is over and I've lined up the work that I need, I go back and address it then.

If you're Top-Rated and think this might be a review you'll need to remove, plan your timing strategically. You have to wait three months between feedback removals; if it's been two and a half months, the moment you leave feedback for the client, his review will be published to your profile--where it will sit out in the open for the next two weeks until you can remove it. It's much better to wait 13 days, respond, and then remove it immediately. s

Another condition for feedback removal is closing ten contracts between removals. Perhaps it's been three months, but you've only closed eight. Leave the potentially negative review in limbo, and find two short-term, fixed-price jobs at the cheapest pay rate you can find. Knock them out of the park, close them out, *then* leave feedback and ask for the negative client review to be removed the moment it goes public.

Responding to Negative Feedback

Either party can end contracts, and occasionally a client triggers that from their end before I have a chance to ask my five-star question. There have been two occasions where this happened, and I found out after I submitted my feedback that I was slightly marked down on some minor area. I went back to the client and asked if I could do anything to make it right, then explained how vital feedback was to my career as a freelancer. In both cases, the client was sympathetic and went back and changed their feedback (you can open this option to them if you want to).

Removing negative feedback. Inevitably, you'll encounter bad feedback that appears on your profile that the client is unwilling to edit or delete. If you're a Top-Rated freelancer, you have the option to remove one piece of feedback from your profile and JSS every three months, as long as you've closed out at least ten contracts since your last feedback removal. There's a specific process that occasionally changes, so I won't outline the steps here, but know that option is available. I'll cover how to become a Top-Rated freelancer, as well as earning other Upwork badges, in the next chapter.

To respond or not to respond. If you're not Top-Rated yet or you've already used a feedback removal and have to wait for your next one, you can respond publicly to the negative feedback. This can be tricky because you need to put yourself in the position of potential future clients and see the whole situation from their eyes, not yours. Depending on the situation, you should handle it in different ways.

If a client leaves a poor star rating but no comment, don't respond. It makes you appear defensive, and future clients will either not take it seriously if there's no comment or ask you about it directly.

Sometimes a client will leave relatively light criticism; think 4 stars and above with a comment that says, "Freelancer was good overall, but could improve communication" or "Great work, but missed the deadline." If this is the case, don't respond. Even if you vehemently disagree with what happened, and possibly even if it's factually incorrect, it appears to be sensible feedback. Publicly defending yourself against reasonable feedback makes you appear argumentative and disagreeable, and clients don't want to hire someone like that. Just accept it, move on, and realize that feedback will soon be swallowed up by new contracts that push it deeper into your history.

Responding correctly. When a client leaves legitimately bad feedback, **ALWAYS** take the high road. If they're attacking you at a level 9 on a 10-point scale, drop back three or four points to a level 5 or 6, maximum. This is your profile, not theirs--don't give them the satisfaction of turning it into a battleground. There are three ways you can lose with your response:

- *Not* responding
- Responding emotionally
- Attacking the client

A future client doesn't know what to do with no response. They might doubt the legitimacy of the bad feedback on your profile, but they don't have anything to go off of. You want to give them some calm, reasonable direction on how to handle this emotional attack against you.

When you respond, *never* use all caps or a single exclamation point. To a large degree, it doesn't matter what either of you says. If the client is screaming and using exclamation points, but you're responding calmly with a "the situation wasn't great, but this part is inaccurate" comment, all any independent reader is going to remember is that you got attacked by a maniac and remained calm.

Keep your response explicitly focused on what they've said about you. If there are aspects to their feedback that are legit, own those, then calmly dispute any attacks against your work ethic or character that are truly undeserved. Be very careful in addressing the client's behavior; you can mention it if it helps explain why they're attacking you, but be extremely conservative here. Your goal is disputing things that are said about you, not returning tit for tat on your profile.

The place for that is on their profile when you leave feedback for them.

How to Leave Negative Feedback

Occasionally it's better to be silent and let sleeping dogs lie, but in this context, those situations are rare. Leaving appropriate feedback is almost always the right thing to do. The vast majority of the time, it's going to be very positive--Upwork excels at attracting and retaining high-quality employers. At some point, however, you'll run into someone who deserves a bad review.

There are two main ways to veer off the straight and narrow path of accurate and appropriate feedback. One is to be passive-aggressive, nailing them in private feedback while refusing to address their behavior in public. The other is to be overly aggressive and attacking them publicly. What you want to do is calmly, reasonably, and briefly explain why other freelancers shouldn't work with them.

It's essential to adopt the mindset that the gig economy in general and Upwork in particular is a community, and it takes collective effort to correct or expel bad behavior. When poor clients and freelancers are allowed to fester, the whole community suffers. When employers and contractors are high-quality, we all win together. I always appreciate it when I can spot a bad client from feedback that other freelancers have left about them. It saves me time, money, and effort because I know not to submit a bid. It preserves the integrity of my profile and JSS because I'm not risking working with a bad client. If the feedback other contractors leave can be beneficial to you, then you owe it to them to do the same in return.

What Appropriate Negative Feedback Looks Like

When you leave bad feedback, it should have three characteristics: it should be calm, fair, and brief. One of the ways you can spot emotional feedback is if it has less than a two-star average. This means the contractor was so upset that they nailed the client in every way they could. There's no way that a client deserves a legitimate one-star rating in Skills, Quality of Work, Availability, Adherence to Schedule, and Communications. One or two areas? Anyone could see that with a crappy client. Three? Perhaps. Four or Five? Naw, you're emotional, and your critique of the client no longer carries weight.

Another indicator of emotional feedback is the use of all caps *at any point* or *any* exclamation points. This is professional business writing, and you need to demonstrate that. Will you be tempted to emphasize what a crappy person this client is? Absolutely. Do they deserve it? Hell yeah, because you're the amazing you, they crossed you, and that means they're two grades shy of Satan himself (don't worry, this is how we all think). Think of it this way, though: every time you display emotion in a negative review, you're chipping away at the foundation of that review in the eyes of every person who will read it.

Finally, be brief. One of the things that makes large amounts of text readable is breaking it into paragraphs; once a chunk of text gets beyond a certain size, it turns into TLDR. TLDR is an acronym that originated in discussion boards and stands for "Too Long, Didn't Read." What you need to understand is that, beyond a certain size, people will take one glance and not even check the first sentence. The review serves literally no purpose at that point. What's tricky is that you can format your thesis-length review into paragraphs when you're typing it, but the moment you submit it, Upwork strips all formatting and turns it into one massive chunk. Limit your feedback to three sentences.

How to Write Negative Feedback

When I discussed how to respond to negative feedback on your profile, I advised you to focus on yourself. You need to flip that narrative here: keep the focus of your three sentences exclusively on them. Don't attack their character, but do address their behavior. Don't deny having faults, but don't address them, either. You're not the topic of conversation here, so leave yourself out of the picture entirely.

As far as content goes, pick the one worst thing they did wrong. They might have been unpleasant, gave you vague instruction, and then made it difficult to get paid, but you don't have the time or space to address all of that in three sentences. Pick the one issue that can be painted most clearly and take three full sentences to develop a picture of a poor client.

Think about a Yelp review for a mechanic. Perhaps this mechanic had a surly attitude, left a grease stain on the driver's side upholstery, scratched the paint on the hood, was three days late in getting the repair done, and by the time it was finally done, he installed the wrong part and ruined your engine. You have every right and legitimate reason to rip this guy a new one with a phonebook-length treatise on his incompetence as a mechanic and human being, but all that would do is guarantee no one would read your review. The guy would keep getting business. What's far more effective is to say this:

> *I took my car to John Doe because it was making a knocking sound. He installed the wrong part and blew my engine up, then refused to replace it. Don't use this guy.*

You just destroyed his business and ignored 80 percent of what he did. You weren't emotional, you didn't attack him, and you didn't rant or rave. You focused on the single worst thing he did, developed it in three sentences, and dropped him.

It's often difficult to do this in the moment, and you shouldn't feel any pressure to do so. Upwork allows you to wait for up to two weeks to leave feedback before publishing it to your profile without input, which means you have plenty of time to cool down. During this time, the review is in limbo and hidden from sight, so no one can see what the client said about you.

Using Negative Feedback to Identify Bad Clients

Sometimes you run across a situation where a lucrative job opportunity presents itself, but the client doesn't have enough feedback to make a decision immediately. In the case below, the client has 3 ½ stars, which is a terrible rating--but it's based on a single review. How

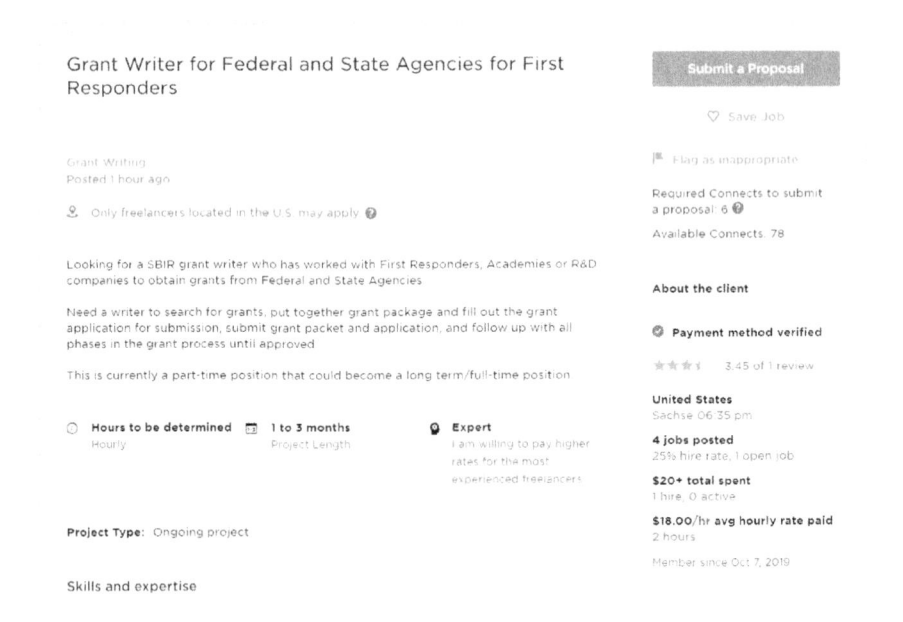

Grant Writer for Federal and State Agencies for First Responders

Grant Writing
Posted 1 hour ago

Only freelancers located in the U.S. may apply

Looking for a SBIR grant writer who has worked with First Responders, Academies or R&D companies to obtain grants from Federal and State Agencies.

Need a writer to search for grants, put together grant package and fill out the grant application for submission, submit grant packet and application, and follow up with all phases in the grant process until approved.

This is currently a part-time position that could become a long term/full-time position

| Hours to be determined | 1 to 3 months | Expert |
| Hourly | Project Length | I am willing to pay higher rates for the most experienced freelancers |

Project Type: Ongoing project

Skills and expertise

Submit a Proposal

Save Job

Flag as inappropriate

Required Connects to submit a proposal: 6
Available Connects: 78

About the client

✓ Payment method verified

★★★☆ 3.45 of 1 review

United States
Sachse 06:35 pm

4 jobs posted
25% hire rate, 1 open job

$20+ total spent
1 hire, 0 active

$18.00/hr avg hourly rate paid
2 hours

Member since Oct 7, 2019

do you know whether this was a terrible individual contract or this client is truly someone you should avoid?

The first thing you should do is scroll down on the job posting to the "Client's recent history" section. Here, you'll find any comments that previous freelancers have left. I typically do this as a matter of course; I've encountered situations before where one or two detailed pieces of negative feedback were enough to deter me from bidding for that client.

```
Client's recent history (1)

Administrative Assistant                         Jan 2020 - Jan 2020
★ ★ ★ 1                                           1.5 hrs @ $18.00/hr
                                                       Billed: $27.00
To freelancer: Sonali N. No feedback given.
```

In this case, there's no comment. We'll need to dig a bit further. The freelancer who left the feedback is hyperlinked here. If you click on her name, Upwork will take you to her profile. What you need to do here is evaluate the quality of the freelancer. Someone who is a low-quality freelancer might be upset that the client held her to high standards, or gave her specific feedback, and she had a terrible attitude. Perhaps the client told her that her work was awful, and she gave him a bad rating as a result.

```
100%                 Administrative Professional            $20.00/hr
Job Success
TOP RATED
                     Analytical and detail-oriented Administrative Assistant experienced in
                     coordinating, planning, and supporting daily operational functions. Offering
$8k+        5        681    expertise in delivering office and administrative support by applying strong
Total Earnings  Total Jobs  Total Hours  organizational, technical, communication, and customer service skills. An
                     outstanding communicator and team player with strong interpersonal skills
                     seeking to thrive in a demanding, deadline-driven environment.
```

In this case, you see someone who is an established freelancer. She's Top Rated, has earned several thousand dollars and has worked 681 hours (or more than four months of full-time labor at 40 hours per week). She has a 100% JSS, so you know that you're dealing with a quality freelancer. Her word can be trusted, and this is a client you should avoid.

It's always possible, of course, that this is inaccurate. Perhaps this is a great client, and something happened that turned the working relationship sour. You don't have all of the details, but you've got to make a call with what you've got. The picture that's being painted here is that you need to avoid bidding on this client's jobs.

Let's say the freelancer had very little experience or a low JSS. If you scroll down on her profile, you'll see the comments that previous clients have made about her. I've seen situations where clients are consistently saying the same thing, and it doesn't paint a pretty picture. Perhaps the freelancer is always late, has poor communication skills, or tends to do a subpar job. If you see this, then you should give the client more benefit of the doubt.

When you have a low-quality client and a suboptimal freelancer, default to not bidding on that job. Upwork has plenty of quality clients, and you don't want to risk your JSS.

Chapter Six Exercise

In this exercise, I want you to review examples of negative client feedback and negative freelancer feedback. To do that, you'll start at your job feed. Scroll until you find a client that has around a four-star rating (anywhere from 3.5 stars to 4.5 stars is good). Ignore all of the clients with 5 stars and all of the clients with no feedback.

Once you've found a job, open it up. Scroll down to the client feedback section and check out the reviews. Here's what I want you to find:

- 5 examples of professional negative feedback about the *client*. These are comments freelancers left for the client. See example 1 below.
- 5 examples of cringeworthy negative feedback about the *client*. These are comments left freelancers left for the client. See example 2 below.
- 5 examples of professional negative feedback about the *freelancer*. These are comments left for the freelancer, and you'll need to click on freelancer links to go back to their profiles. See example 3 below.
- 5 examples of cringeworthy negative feedback about the *freelancer*. These are comments left for the freelancer, and you'll need to click on freelancer links to go back to their profiles. See example 4 below.

Take screenshots of each of these and put them in an album where you can flip through and review them. Ask yourself what kind of assumptions you make about the person *leaving the feedback*. Do you assume that whoever wrote the review has a lot of class and professionalism, or does it sound like someone you want to stay away from? Ask yourself what kind of assumptions you make about the person *the feedback was about*. Does this feedback make you want to avoid them? Do you disregard it?

Seeing examples of feedback and how they impact your impressions of both the person who left it and the one who receives it is invaluable.

If you have a contract go bad, you might be angry enough to spit fire and absolutely want to ream the client in your feedback to them. Remember, though--other clients can find these comments, and you need to be aware of how you're perceived.

Example 1: Professional feedback about a client

> SEO Content Writer & Editor
> ★ ★ ★ ★ Although this project wasn't quite what I expected and the preparation part was a bit lengthy, I would work with this client again. Overall he was friendly and very good at communicating. less
> To freelancer: Shamontiel V. No feedback given.
>
> Feb 2017 - Feb 2017
> 1 hrs @ $20.00/hr
> Billed: $20.00

This is a perfectly structured negative feedback comment about a client. The freelancer commented about the project itself, then explained that the client was solid. Based on this, I would know to ask a lot of clarifying questions of the client upfront to make sure I understood the work scope, but I wouldn't be afraid to bid. As a client, seeing this kind of feedback would make me *more* likely to hire this freelancer, because she's obviously professional.

Example 2: Cringeworthy feedback about a client

> ★ NOT RECOMMENDED AT ALL, Jeremiah is the client who himself came for a job with his own timelines of week only to complete the project which I accepted and quoted him the price accordingly but when he started the work then he get it from a week to more than a month with loads of work without increasing the price and whenever I asked him to set an ETA to finish the job he always give me a shut-up call by saying that never ask me an ETA and he wanted me to work as long as he want without even increasing the price. He is totally unprofessional and sets his own rules for his jobs !!!! less

This review consists of only two sentences, and the first might set some kind of record. Using all caps, multiple exclamation points, and poor grammar indicates that this was an emotionally-driven review from someone who doesn't value professionalism very highly. I wouldn't count this feedback against the client at all. Never, ever leave feedback like this.

Example 3: Professional feedback about a freelancer

⭐ **1.00** Aug 2019 - Nov 2019

Took the job and said she would do it, but never completed it and never explained why she can't do it or provide any explanation for delay.

This feedback is short and to the point. Although you can tell the client isn't pleased, this isn't an emotional response. It's well thought out, reasonable, and indicates a freelancer you don't want to work with.

Example 4: Cringeworthy feedback about a freelancer

⭐⭐ **2.50** Mar 2020 - Apr 2020

Turned me off upwork...no longer interested in working with upwork!

When you blame the entire platform and millions of freelancers based on a single contract with an individual freelancer, you're emotionally reacting. I wouldn't hold this review against the freelancer.

CHAPTER SEVEN

Thriving

There's quite a bit of difference between having a full-time job as a freelancer and approaching it as a career. When someone sees freelancing as a job, they tend to be passive, reactive, and drift. There's nothing wrong with this, particularly if you know freelancing is acting as a filler position between jobs, and you're actively searching for something different. However, if you're going to spend any length of time in this arena, you should treat it as a career move, even if you don't plan on being an independent contractor forever.

Having a freelancing career can involve aspects of project management, accounting, marketing & advertising, human resources, and sales, in addition to your actual line of work. Even the projects themselves can be an excellent opportunity to explore various areas that are new and intriguing. A year ago, I was having a conversation with James, a freelancing buddy of mine. He asked me a question that, in any other area of life, might have seemed odd. "When you tell people you're a freelancer," he said, "what do you tell them that you do??"

In Chapter 1, I mention how I started freelancing by writing resumes, then moved on to proofreading, then copywriting, blog writing, research articles, research projects, various areas of academic writing editing, ghostwriting, and finally ended up as a project manager. If you divided my work into primary roles, you'd find at least three completely different jobs: writing, researching, and project management. Let's say I had a passion for graphic design. I could teach myself how to do this, then create a specialized profile as a graphic designer. While I bid for jobs to pay my bills as an expert writer, I could simultaneously bid for work as an entry-level designer, then explore a possible career renovation.

Viewing what you do as a career simply means that you're intentional about every aspect of it. Even if you're not trying to get to the point where you start an agency, employ other freelancers, or substantially increase your pay rate, you can pursue self-development. The lessons you learn here can position you to re-enter the "normal" workforce in virtually any position and capacity you choose.

Getting Paid

This is the most enjoyable part of being a freelancer. The timelines for getting paid vary slightly depending on whether it's an hourly or fixed-price contract. For hourly work, the billing cycle runs from Monday at 00:00 midnight UTC through Sunday at 23:59 UTC. Once the period ends, freelancers have twelve hours to make adjustments; then, clients have through the following Friday to review the work and request any changes. These hours are automatically invoiced to the client and paid out by Upwork ten days after the billing cycle ends.

Fixed-price contracts and manual pay adjustments (e.g., a client can choose to give you a bonus) become available five calendar days after the client approves payment.

You'll set up at least one payment mechanism with Upwork when you get started. The site currently offers four options:

- **Instant Pay**, where funds are immediately sent to your bank account when you request a withdrawal. This costs $2 per transaction.
- **Direct Deposit/ACH**, where the funds are automatically forwarded to your US bank account for free. It can take 3-5 business days to receive the funds.
- **PayPal**, where Upwork charges $1 per withdrawal, and PayPal may charge additional fees.
- **Wire transfer**, which costs $30 per wire and takes up to 7 business days for the funds to process.

I recommend setting a direct deposit up as your default method, then being aware of the other mechanisms, and using them on an as-needed basis. You can set up a payment schedule for quarterly, monthly, twice per month, or weekly. You have to earn a minimum balance of $100 for funds to transfer out via direct deposit. Before any funds can be withdrawn, you have to complete a W-9 and submit it to Upwork.

Maintaining a Consistent, Stable Workflow

Think of contract work as a train with a series of connected cars. There's a bit of separation between each of the cars, and if the engine is pulling at a consistent speed (regardless of whether that is fast or slow), the cars move along smoothly. If the locomotive is continuously stopping and starting, though, the cars jerk back and forth, causing damage to the goods and passengers in addition to the cars themselves. A tremendous amount of fuel is burned to get where the train needs to go because the start/stop motion is incredibly wasteful.

One of the biggest struggles I have as a freelancer is maintaining a consistent, stable workflow. It's a constant balancing act that I get right sometimes and wrong occasionally. The more I strive to perfect it, the closer I get to consistently predicting how busy my week will be, how much work I need to bid for next week, and how to balance short-term and long-term contracts.

The critical term here is balance. Long-term work involves more stability but at the sacrifice of flexibility. At some point, you essentially become a remote employee without the paid vacation, health insurance, and 401k. Short term work is exciting, challenging, and fresh, but it's also less consistent. Having a mix of the two is essential to ensure that you're balancing stability with flexibility and excitement with consistency.

The benefits of diversifying. One way to emphasize long-term stability as a freelancer is to avoid putting all of your eggs in one basket. I recommend having a minimum of three long-term contracts at any given point; you can never tell when a company's priorities or budget will shift, and your contract comes to a sudden end. This isn't a bad thing; it's the nature of freelancing. If you're using a rope with three major strands and one gets cut, you're not going to fall very far; the other two will support you while searching for a replacement. However, if you're dependent on one client for all, or even the majority, of your income, you're creating an employee dynamic without the perks.

I recommend developing a baseline of long-term contracts that comprise the majority of your income. This maximizes the amount of time you spend working and minimizes the time you have to commit to bidding, which is unpaid. However, you need to maintain a consistent stream of short-term jobs. Even if you only have one at a time, then look for another when the first is complete, keeping yourself in the bidding and job-finding mindset is critical to long-term success. When I stay out of the bidding game too long, I find that I'm reticent to jump back in. I lose confidence in my bidding, interview, and negotiation skills and subconsciously avoid doing it, which leads to unused hours that could be filled with billable work if I'd planned ahead.

Maintenance bidding. One of the things I make myself do is bid for one job per day, even if my plate is 100 percent full. There are two reasons for this. The first is that I'm keeping my skills sharp and maintaining a finger on the pulse of the market, so I can instantly pivot and bid at a high level when I need work. The second is slowly pushing the envelope on my pay rate. When I bid for new work but have a full plate, I can set prices as high as I'd like to--the worst that can happen is I don't get the job. When I do get a job, however, it's at an extremely competitive wage. I've settled on $85 an hour as my baseline; that's where I can consistently pick up a full workload with my skill set. I'll submit full-load bids at $95 to $125 an hour, and I lose those the vast majority of the time. When I win them, however, it's like getting a mid-month bonus.

Knowing how much work you need is easy when you have forty hours of hourly-rate contracts. However, if this isn't the case, you have to estimate the amount of time it takes to perform each task. This is where tracking your work gives you an advantage. I keep a whiteboard on my wall that serves as a living tracker of how much work I have and when it's due. My goal is always to live in the planning stage for next week; if I'm bidding for work I'll accomplish this week, I'm behind the curve. If I'm bidding for jobs two weeks out, I'm looking too far out for what most clients would be satisfied with and setting myself up to disappoint them. Even if we agree on a deadline two weeks out, most employers aren't looking at contract work that far out, and by the time that day comes, they've subconsciously gotten impatient and *feel* that you're late, even if you aren't. When you're operating at a solid tempo, you're living in next week.

Mixing contract types. Leveraging contract types against each other also comes into play with pay models. I find that if I mix fixed-price jobs and hourly work, the combination makes me better at each. Getting paid at a fixed-price makes me watch my time more carefully because whether a task is profitable or not depends on me. It makes me more efficient. However, I do some of my best creative work when I'm getting paid on an hourly basis because I can relax my focus and think. This pay model makes me more effective at my job. Combining mechanisms that bolster my efficiency and effectiveness work continually with each other to raise the bar on my performance.

Enjoying Contract Perks

Contracts offer various perks that you can ethically take advantage of, and they fall into two primary categories: tangible and intangible.

Tangible benefits. One of my current contracts is for an IT company that specializes in certification exam preparation. I don't have an interest in an IT career, but I do project management professionally, and one of the cert prep courses they offer is for a highly valued PM certification. I asked my supervisor if he would authorize a free trial subscription while I worked for them; my pitch was based on the fact that the more I learned about their product offerings firsthand, the better my writing would be. It didn't cost them a thing, and he authorized it, providing me with several hundred dollars worth of education.

A past client ran several successful keto sites and regularly published recipes and various diet resources. I started the diet and asked if I could get copies of their paid meal plans and cookbooks, which he happily forwarded to me. Since all I needed were the PDFs, it didn't cost him a thing, better equipped me for the work he wanted me to do, and gave me something I wanted for free.

Intangible benefits. Some of the more intangible benefits revolve around gaining knowledge and making career contacts. At the start of my career, I had a client who wanted to put together a blog on all of the ways you could save on airfare. She sent me a bunch of resources with interviews from airline personnel that talked about the ins and outs of billing models, how and where airlines published last-minute cut-rate fares to fill seats, and how to maximize on pricing errors caused by computer glitches. Although I signed an NDA and can't share that knowledge with anyone, you can bet your butt that I've leveraged it for my own use.

My LinkedIn network has swelled as a result of freelancing. Every time I have a successful encounter with a client, I add him or her on LinkedIn. Maintaining this thread of contact has resulted in repeat work from the same customers and word-of-mouth recommendations that developed into future contracts. I held a substantial role with a large company for a year and a half, and I know that if I ever need a job, I can shoot out three or four emails and have a job at that corporation within the month.

Don't hesitate to think about how a contract can benefit you beyond the immediate payment. In fact, this should always be on your mind. Early in my career, I wanted to get my name on bylines to promote my skillset. I found a job posting for ghostwriting the cover article for the inaugural edition of a brand-new magazine in a rapidly growing industry. The other bids ranged from $300 to $500--mine was $5. My cover letter's opening line began with: "My bid is an actual amount, and here's why I'll execute for that amount…" I told him that, in exchange for writing the article nearly for free, I wanted to be named as the author or co-author of the article. We had great chemistry, he hired me, and my name was published online and in print. I've since used that experience and publication to pull in thousands of dollars of work.

Always act ethically. Although there are ways you can unethically leverage insider knowledge and contract benefits, this is always a short-term choice that cuts your legs out from under you. Never act unethically. There are innumerable benefits to be gained that are completely above-board, and clients will often actively encourage you to use them.

Earning the Top-Rated Badge

If you're going to spend several months or more as a freelancer on Upwork, gaining the Top-Rated badge (and subsequent, higher badges) should be a priority. It can't be purchased and must be earned. The badge unlocks several benefits that will enhance what you can do on the platform and accelerate your career if you use it correctly.

Earning a Top-Rated status requires meeting seven criteria:

- A current Job Success Score of 90% or higher *(see Chapter Three)*
- Maintained Rising Talent status or a Job Success Score of at least 90% for at least 13 of the last 16 weeks
- A 100% complete profile *(see Chapter Three)*
- 12-month earnings of at least $1,000 *(which means you don't have to be a full-time freelancer to earn this; you just have to be active)*
- Up-to-date availability *(see Chapter Three)*

- An account in good standing with no recent account holds
- Activity on the platform (proposal, accepted invitation, or earnings) in the past 90 days

Upwork has done an excellent job of choosing metrics that are easy to attain if you're even slightly active (e.g., pulling in $1,000 a year and submitting a job bid once every three months), while tying them into performance metrics that actually matter. Upwork does a phenomenal job supporting its higher-level contractors but doesn't offer a tremendous amount of support if you're new. Once you've reached Top-Rated status, you'll have access to premier customer support over the phone and via chat, which can be tremendously useful.

One of the benefits I covered in Chapter Six was the ability to remove negative feedback from your profile periodically. Now, you don't get to Top-Rated status by receiving a lot of negative reviews, but if you're around for long enough, you're inevitably going to butt heads with a client. Having the ability to remove a one-off piece of client feedback is invaluable.

It's easier to find work as a Top-Rated freelancer, and it's more tangible than the nifty little icon on your profile that highlights your storied history of grandeur. Clients can employ a filter when searching for freelancers to invite to a job that narrows the list to contractors who have reached this status. Being Top-Rated includes you in more filter options, giving you a higher chance of being discovered, invited, and finding work.

Developing Symbiotic Relationships with Other Freelancers

Although working as an independent contractor does involve quite a bit of independence, it doesn't have to mean being alone. In fact, the more closely you network with other contractors, the better off you'll be.

There are three types of people with whom you should network. I already mentioned how doing a good job for clients can result in word-of-mouth recommendations and more work, but it's also important to connect with other freelancers--both those who can be seen as competitors and those who work in fundamentally different industries.

Working with "competitors." It's tempting to look at other contractors who have similar skill sets and see them as competition. To some degree, they are, of course, but they also help create a healthier community and can be allies in many respects. Consider it from this perspective: I'm a writer, but the more quality writers that are part of the Upwork community, the more clients will see Upwork as the place to go when you need a quality writer. That creates more work for everyone, allowing for increased selection and specialization. As writers specialize, they fan out among the hundreds of different unique styles, subject matter, and niches that writing has to offer, which actually *decreases* the competition for my particular skill set simultaneously with more work being brought in. It's a win for everyone.

That's just a healthy community, but symbiosis can also be achieved through direct connections with peers in the same industry. I can't tell you the number of times I've had clients ask if I can take care of a particular writing task, and I knew someone who was a better fit, so I pointed the client to them. This creates two advantages for me: first, I develop a reputation with customers as someone who is a resource they should keep around, leading to more work. Second, those other writers return the favor, which also leads to more work.

Emphasizing diversity. A similar dynamic is at play when you develop more connections with freelancers in completely distinct fields with no inherent relationship to yours. In one of my contracts, I worked closely with a graphic designer, and we became good friends. I've leveraged his expertise in at least three other contracts where the client wanted a writer with accompanying graphic design. Because I knew someone with whom I could work closely and was familiar enough with his rates to include an approximate quote with my own, I beat out other writers who didn't have this kind of connection.

I've been contacted to interview for jobs out of the blue, only to discover later that the invitation wasn't so random after all. I've made friends who are administrative assistants, and when their supervisors discovered a need for a writer, their immediate response was, "I know a guy…"

One of the services I offer after you've read this book is the opportunity to join a small group of other freelancers. I put everyone together in groups of five to eight, and each member of the group has a different skillset and is at a similar point in their freelancing journey. This is your first direct introduction to networking; together, you can share lessons learned, tips and tricks, and then leverage each others' expertise to build a foundation for a successful career.

Using the Upwork Community

Upwork provides a tremendous level of support to established freelancers with high JSS. However, they provide substantially less support for brand-new freelancers. This is intentional: the platform hosts 12 million contractors. If you've ever worked in a customer support role, you know that many questions can be answered if someone is willing to explore the resources that the company offers. Upwork is an intuitive platform and has many resources to answer questions you might have, particularly if it's something that starts with "How."

If you have a question that starts with "Why," you'll need to go to the Upwork Community (community.upwork.com). In many ways, this functions as a platform-specific Reddit discussion board where you can find answers to numerous questions. Beyond the peer resources available, Upwork specialists also frequent the boards. If they see inaccurate information being passed around or find that someone has asked a question no one can answer, you'll often see them chiming in.

I know, it would be nice if we had our own concierge on call to give us all of the information available, but Upwork Community is a close second. I've actually never asked a question there, but I use it frequently to browse what other people are asking and the answers being posted.

Upwork also uses this as a forum to post announcements about new platform features or policies. You'll want to check this on a weekly basis, at least, to make sure you're up to speed on anything that might affect you. There is also a host of reference material that can get you up to speed on various platform features.

Finally, you'll find a Community Bot named "Data" that is an automated text feature. This will help guide you to the right answer quickly and efficiently. If you can't find at least a general explanation with this feature, you might want to create a new post and ask your question there.

Working with Agencies

The topic of agencies is a book unto itself, but I'll introduce the overall concept here. Essentially, an agency is an online business comprised of multiple freelancers and hosted entirely on Upwork. Agencies offer a variety of skill sets in a single location, which can be useful for clients who have needs across different areas or are constantly changing.

The agency is awarded the contract and then assigns the work to its freelancers. The client pays the agency directly, and then the agency pays the freelancers off-platform.

Some clients prefer freelancers to agencies, and there are various filters clients can leverage to focus on individuals. Other clients prefer the simplicity of handing off any task to an agency project manager and not having to worry about it. There are pros and cons to each. If you're advanced enough on the Upwork platform to manage multiple freelancers, consider starting your own business and bidding for more complex projects.

Chapter Seven Exercise

Well, here we are: the last exercise. I've covered a tremendous amount of material, and remembering everything is going to be a challenge, let alone applying it! This two-part capstone exercise will help consolidate everything and prioritize what you need to do.

Step One: Create three SMART goals

A SMART Goal is one that's Specific, Measurable, Attainable, Realistic, and Time-bound (i.e., it has a specific date). Perhaps you want to achieve a certain pay rate within six months, or move to full-time freelancing by a specific point. Getting there is going to require that you use this book in its entirety and focus your efforts in a targeted direction. Here are a few examples:

- *Land my first Upwork contract by December 10th.*
- *Get three five-star feedbacks from clients by March 17th.*
- *Have 40 hours of contracted work per week by September 25th.*
- *Earn at least $50 an hour on two different contracts by April 15th.*

- *Earn my Top Rated badge by June 1st.*
- *Total $25k in earnings by November 2nd.*

The more specific your goals are, the more likely you are to achieve them. You should also post these somewhere you'll see and read them regularly. Reviewing your goals daily makes it seven times more likely that you'll achieve them. They're always on your mind, which causes you to subconsciously orient even the small actions of your day to help get you there.

I want you to create three SMART goals. A simple goal you achieve is much better than a lofty one that doesn't take you anywhere, so don't be afraid to start small. I'd recommend starting with one that you can accomplish in two weeks, one that will take you a month, and one that will take two months. As you accomplish them, create new, bigger ones to keep propelling you forward.

Step Two: Partner for success

The single most important piece of workout equipment you can have is a partner (just don't tell them that they're "equipment"). A partner will keep you accountable to push when you don't feel like it and will inspire you with their successes. Freelancing is no different. You'll have some discouragements along the way, and it helps if you can vent to someone who knows what you're talking about and can empathize or has overcome this kind of problem, and you can look to for encouragement.

If you don't currently know anyone on Upwork, there are two options. The first is simple: ask some of your friends to join. Remember what I said at the beginning of the book--I think everyone should have an Upwork profile. It doesn't matter whether your friends are employed full-time or have been out of a job for six months, there's a spot for them.

The trick is that you only want to pick people who will inspire you. Don't ask friends who will end up being dead weight that you have to carry; you don't need that in your life. Approach your successful friends, the ones who aren't afraid of hard work, the people who are continually seeking to better themselves. Those are the partners you want.

I also offer a Peer Mentorship Group on my website: www.Upwork-Masters.com. With this option, you'll be paired with 6 to 8 other freelancers in various industries; if you're an administrative assistant, you might get matched with a writer, a graphic designer, and a computer programmer. I structure it this way so you know you're not competing against anyone in your group for jobs, but you're all working toward similar goals on the same platform.

Over eight weeks, you'll chat regularly and meet with an experienced mentor who can point you in the right direction when you have questions. You'll network and leverage each other's knowledge and experiences. Instead of having to make mistakes yourself, you'll get 6 or 8 times the experience in the same period.

Regardless of which you choose, **find partners**.

This book has given you the knowledge you need to get there. Making goals will set your course, and partners will keep you moving toward it even when you get discouraged. With a bit of effort, you can reach your dreams, whatever they are.

Epilogue

The Importance of Tenacity

I found Upwork in December of 2017. I'd lost my job a few months prior and, by the time I was hired into another position, had burned through my savings. I'll never forget the moment I looked at my first paycheck from my new job and realized that it wouldn't be enough to feed my four kids. I remember that feeling of desperation, loneliness, and the weight of my world on my shoulders. I'd finalized my divorce a year prior and looked around at the financial wreckage of my life. I'd sold everything I owned that someone would buy. My credit card was nearly maxed, and I'd been denied a personal loan. I was living thousands of miles from where I'd grown up, with no friends or family to help. I was utterly alone.

Over the past two years, I'd tried to make ends meet in a variety of ways. I returned to college full-time on the GI Bill primarily to get the housing stipend that came with it--and that's how my rent was paid. I tried to start a business seven different times--it failed on each attempt. Between my erratic retail schedule and parenting time for four small kids, I was averaging four hours of sleep a night and simply didn't have space for much more, and my schedule prevented me from getting any other part-time job I considered.

I finally swallowed my pride and looked into government support. I found out that I was in one of those holes between programs: my gross income was too high, but because I was passing so much on to my ex and kids, the net that I had left wasn't enough to pay my bills.

That was when I seriously considered cashing in my life insurance policy.

Looking back on it now, it's hard to emotionally realize the depth of the despair that characterized my life at that point. I had nothing, and the little I did have wasn't enough to meet my needs. I needed a chance, even if it was the smallest chance in the world. In a moment perfectly orchestrated by fate, that's when a friend introduced me to the world of freelance writing. I remembered a site he had told me about, called "Upwork." He was someone I'd served with in the Air Force, and he had dabbled in writing on the side. At that point, I was ready to take any opportunity that was legal, so I jumped at the chance.

I recognized that this offered the flexibility I needed: I could work as hard as possible for as long as was necessary, and I could do it from home. That's when Upwork required freelancers to apply before joining the platform then, and I applied--and was rejected. So I reworked my profile and applied again--and was denied. Half a dozen times, this repeated itself. I didn't give up because I couldn't. I didn't have anywhere else to go. Failure wasn't an option. Finally, after the sixth attempt, I was accepted to the platform.

I didn't know what my skills were. I didn't know how to describe myself, how to write a cover letter, and had absolutely no idea what to charge for my services. What was I worth on an hourly basis? How in the world was I supposed to know how to bid for fixed-price jobs? What clients were good, and which ones should I avoid? The learning curve was steep, and honestly, overwhelming. But again, I didn't have a choice. I had to make this work, or my kids weren't going to be able to eat.

I went balls to the wall, bidding for jobs in the morning before I went to work, then interviewing with clients on my lunch break. At night, I'd come home, grab a bite to eat, and then write until I fell asleep. It took a couple of weeks before I felt I was starting to make any headway, but one day, it was as if my spinning tires finally caught traction, and away I went. Clients turned into repeat customers and then into referrals. I'd reworked my profile and cover letter a score of times. I was finally figuring out how to use the platform, how to bid effectively, and how to define my skill set.

I woke up and wrote for hours before my kids began to stir at 6 am. I stayed up until midnight more times than I could count. I logged hours every single day before and after my full-time job, then poured myself into it on the weekends. I submitted bids and quotes during my lunch break; when work was slow, I'd pull up a document or open my notebook and begin throwing words onto a page.

Within 12 weeks, I was bringing home more from my side gig than I was at my regular job. I began to wonder if I could make this a full-time job, so one week, I put in far more bids than was usual for me. Within three days, I'd contracted 80 hours of work per week. I had my answer, but the decision was far from easy. I had a stable position as a state employee at a nationally-ranked university. My job wasn't going anywhere: it had health insurance, a retirement plan, promotion potential--everything that appealed to me as a single dad with four kids. At the same time, I recognized that when opportunity knocks, you damned well better be ready to answer.

So I quit my job and became a full-time freelancer. Eight months after I started at $25 an hour, I landed my first contract for $125 an hour. Two and a half years later, I wouldn't change a thing.

There have been difficult times, for sure. I've gone through five separate "droughts" where I couldn't land a contract to save my life. Each of these lasted for ten days to two weeks, but every single time, they've passed, and I've picked right back up. Sometimes I had to adjust my rates; others, I had to change the kinds of jobs I was bidding on or the cover letter I was using. Occasionally, I just had to push through. What I've learned, though, is that if you're tenacious enough, you can always make a living working for yourself.

When I tell people that it took me twelve weeks from the first contract I won to the point where I was making more as a "part-time" freelancer than a full-time executive assistant, they tend to picture something different than what happened. When I ask them what they imagine, they tend to paint a picture of someone putting in five to ten hours a week, when it's convenient, and going to bed when he gets tired. They don't picture someone putting in forty hours of effort on top of the fifty hours he already put in at work. They don't see the gallons of coffee I consumed just to keep my eyes open long enough to crank out another few paragraphs. They can't feel the tears that poured down my cheeks or the sobs wracking my body as I broke down from the stress, then pulled myself back together and got back on my computer to write some more.

It's much easier to focus on the fact that it took me twelve weeks to go from a single, trial writing job to eighty hours a week of contract work. The picture is much happier when you think about the fact that eight months after I pulled my first job at $25 an hour, I won a contract for $125 an hour. You'll find it more pleasant to imagine yourself in my shoes when earning six figures went from being a pipe dream to an accepted reality.

The good news is that I can circumvent a lot of that pain and effort for you. This book is an on-ramp to the freelancing interstate, where my journey more closely resembled ramming a four-wheel-drive through a barely established path in the woods. I paid attention, learned the lessons, and can pass that knowledge on to you.

Participating in the gig economy is a nearly perfect solution, regardless of where you are in life. If you want a bit of supplemental income on the side to pay down a few bills or save for a vacation, land a job a week. If you're looking for full-time opportunities, you can make that happen, and the amount of money you pull in is limited only by your willingness to work for it. If you just want an option in your back pocket in case your industry hits a few snags, contract work is a perfect fit.

The COVID-19 pandemic has introduced a tremendous amount of uncertainty into the lives of tens of millions of people in the United States alone. Jobs that seemed secure are now anything but, and those of us with kids are wondering how we can work full-time and simultaneously adapt to a closed or hybrid school situation. There's never been a better time to expand your options than now.

Whatever your goals and wherever you are in life, having the option to freelance is something I'd highly recommend, even if it's just a backup option because of the current economic uncertainty. It can take weeks for unemployment benefits to start up and months to find a replacement job. The average time it takes from a job being posted to when a contractor is hired and starting work varies between 48 and 72 hours, depending on the platform.

Freelancing equals freedom. Go out there and get it.

About the Author

Josh Burnett has worked in a broad range of jobs. From construction worker to structural firefighter, he knows what it means to get his hands dirty. As a college professor and professional writer, he's harnessed the power of his mind to make a living. Now, in his breakout book, Josh shares the secrets to his most lucrative and enjoyable career yet.

Printed in Great Britain
by Amazon